THERE'S ONLY "I" IN TEAM

Lisa —
You are a tremendous, I am brilliant human + I am so lucky to have you as my friend! go get em, genius! Warmly,

3/500

THERE'S ONLY "I" IN TEAM

A.M. SPADAFORE, PH.D.

NEW DEGREE PRESS

COPYRIGHT © 2021 A.M. SPADAFORE, PH.D.

THERE'S ONLY "I" IN TEAM

ISBN

978-1-63730-651-2 *Paperback*
978-1-63730-734-2 *Kindle Ebook*
978-1-63730-925-4 *Digital Ebook*

To your genius

CONTENTS

———

INTRODUCTION: AERIAL, CANARIES, AND "WEIRD SCIENCE"

———

The scene is dark, dusky, and sexy. The stage is bathed in moody lighting, with a faint smoke rising from the floor.

A translucent, enormous goblet of water, perfectly sized for a giant, sits in the center, nestled within an equally immense cast-iron stand. It's gigantic enough for two adult humans to swim in mermaid-style.

For now, it represents anticipation, filled with crisp aqua water just begging to be dipped into.

While the overall atmosphere is dim and misty, we know that a sensuous and steamy playfulness is imminent, given the muted jewel tone colors being beamed across the stage.

The curtain is about to rise on Cirque du Soleil's *Amaluna*. Expectantly, we wait to be entertained.

After we've spent just a little bit too much time in this dreamy and delectable state of longing and desire, the "heavens" open and a beautiful, lithe nymph appears.

Hovering effortlessly fifty feet in the air, suspended only by the elegant crook of her neck, she gracefully leans backwards into a thin, metal circle attached to an unseen ceiling from an unobtrusive black rope.

In perfect rhythm with the pouty strains of a solo electric guitar, she elegantly sweeps around the stage in a glorious aquamarine and crystal leotard: a vision of sprightly blonde curls, and ripped, powerful muscle.

Her succession of aerial tricks continues apace—with only her strength, the rope, and a thin metal ring separating her from certain death—as the guitar gives way to an intense electronica soundtrack.

She flits above and around the immense goblet, transporting you to a faraway land where Tinker Bell exists and the typical rules of gravity do not apply.

As she hovers just above, the stage itself begins to turn gently, gliding in soft motion like the world's most erotic merry-go-round.

She continues to touch ground, ever-so-gently teasing us with her humanity before her rope raises her far above the audience. It transports her repeatedly to a netherworld of suspension between the Earth and the heavens, which none of us transfixed ordinaries will ever get to visit.

This gorgeous character, resplendent in her outrageous abilities, is still a human. She is still subject to the laws of physics and human nature, and all the other typical annoyances on earth.

In addition to her truly heart-stopping performance, what transports her—and us—to this magical place night after night, performance after performance, is a delicately performed illusion.

She appears on the stage solo. Her beauty, grace, and talent stand alone, an elegant vision of perfection with one divinity at the center.

But she is not alone. There are hundreds, if not thousands, of individuals involved in this performance. The acrobat herself, those working behind the scenes, and even the audience, all interdependent in creating this exotic spectacle.

She is just one part of an amazing team of individuals—a team who must get everything right at exactly the precise moment to ensure that our elfin heroine is safe after each flight.

Musicians play the soundtrack to her live performance. Dozens of crew members operate the elaborate rigging necessary for her to perform her tricks on stage with surgical precision.

Producers, lighting experts, makeup and hair professionals, and costumers—they have also contributed to this performance. Her fellow performers wait backstage, anticipating their opportunity to provide their immense talents to the show.

She is a part of a huge team. Obviously, they literally impact her performance. We can easily see and know this impact when we think about it (although we don't know everything that is occurring in their lives which may be impacting their performance that particular evening).

This is her "team." They travel together, support each other, and perform together. They may begin each performance with a team meal, or a team blessing/prayer, or a team "high-five."

In a troupe like Cirque du Soleil, teamwork is everything. Teamwork not only determines the ultimate outcome of a show and wows audiences, who rave to their friends that they *must see this new show*: teamwork determines the ongoing financial solvency of the organization they work for.

Teamwork is a critical factor in performers' safety. Their work has life and death implications. They are masters at their craft, but they can truly only be as spectacular as the rest of the team around them.

Yet your view from the seats is focused on the singular performer on stage. You don't see "behind the scenes." In a performance, that is necessary for the illusion.

This illusion is not just on the stage—it persists in the business world and life in general. We think of ourselves as members of a society, as well as members of many organizations, groups, and teams. We believe our outcomes and our thinking is mostly if not singularly in our control. We don't see this for the illusion that it is.

The performer doesn't exist in a vacuum, and neither do we. She is the only person on the stage, but she is just one of thousands of individuals in that network of people within that venue.

They are all inevitably affecting her performance, no matter how talented she is on her own.

What if our work lives, and our personal lives, were more like that Cirque du Soleil performance than we realized?

What about the critical amount of behind-the-scenes action (much like the cast and crew backstage) that we don't consider when assessing ours and others' behaviors in situations?

There's more.

What if there's even another, more invisible illusion that we can't see in our own brains, and in the brains of others?

This illusion is that we control our own brains, and that we master what happens inside our brains as we interact with others.

Neuroscience released in the last several years indicates that we are more affected by the presence of others than we realize. We may not be explicitly aware of it happening, but each of us experience "deposits" and "withdrawals" in our bodies as a function of the people who surround us, and who impact us with their behavior (Barrett 2020).

Our brains, as the master controllers of our body systems, continuously attempt to control this positive and negative sum balance. However, the brain only operates this delicate balancing act based on its best guesses and predictions.

Furthermore, this impact by others is mediated by our own prior experiences. Some of us may experience the "deposits" and "withdrawals" differently, based on our personal and family histories.

The people around us and on our teams may impact us and our performance far more than we realize, not just by what they do or produce, but by their physical and mental states as we spend time with them.

We know our flying heroine needs an alert rigging operator to keep her safe as she glides around the stage. As we'll see, her performance is affected by the anxiety level inside those around her, impacting her as she delivers her death-defying act night after night.

Shifting from the stage to the office, this research has significant implications for our performance at work.

We may be quick to point fingers when things don't go as planned, but we might not really know what else is going on that has contributed to a less-than-ideal outcome at work both within ourselves or within others.

Like the Cirque du Soleil stage, we don't *see* what is happening backstage or what happened before the performer took the stage. We don't *see* what is going on inside the performer's body and her brain. But it's all impacting her and her performance and everyone else's performance.

Whether you are wearing a leotard or a suit, it doesn't matter. Every human on a team, or in any other context with other humans (groups, organizations, societies, and families) *has been* and *is being* impacted by their environments and the humans around them.

Therefore, I propose a completely different way of thinking about ourselves and others in the contexts of teams, organizations, and other networks of humans.

WHY YOU SHOULD CARE

Organizations spend more than $82 billion a year on training alone, not to mention the costs of coaching, books, and other internal and external resources to help their top talent work most effectively as individuals and on teams (Training Industry Report 2020).

Teamwork is a business problem. Teams are a fact of life in organizations. We need other people to do our best work. But the presence of others can often *prevent us* from doing our best work in ways we cannot immediately see.

This paradox impairs organizational results and serves as a barrier to the vital human creativity, innovation, and ingenuity that is necessary for problem solving and survival in a complex and competitive business world.

Working with the most senior individuals in the world's most competitive industries, I've repeatedly seen an alarming dynamic: the very top talent is recruited to join superstar teams in name-brand organizations. They must then navigate the challenging paradox of retaining their superstar talent while contributing their best to their team and organization.

Far more frequently, world-class performers come together in a team and produce less-than-stellar results. The superstars get on each other's nerves and get in each other's way. Each person's world-class performance capabilities can become diminished.

Frustrated and anxious (and made even more so by the fact that they *know* they could do better), they may overly control, blame, compete, or undermine each other in subtle ways.

They might even check out, neglect their responsibility, or become overly fixated on another person as a way of attempting to deal with this frustration and anxious energy.

This often produces even more frustration and anxious energy, in the proverbial downward spiral.

Rather than a stellar Cirque du Soleil performance, each person involved in or adjacent to such unhealthy team dynamics feels more like they have a front seat to a plain ole circus.

This is where I come in...

A LITTLE BIT ABOUT ME

I'm a professional who is excited about updating our thinking about human interaction, particularly within organizational and business settings.

Some people run screaming away from complexity. I'm fascinated by the intricacy and sophistication of human brains and behavior and the challenge of helping others comprehend this complexity in an insightful and entertaining manner.

In my work, I've come to some preliminary conclusions:

- I think a cause-effect way of thinking about human performance ("He is a [label]," or "He is the problem," or "She caused this problem,") is unsophisticated and unrealistic and has no place in world-class business operations. That said, I do appreciate the convenience of thinking this way (which, as we'll see, is a huge part of its lasting appeal).

- I'm more interested in *what's really happening* in these situations, which, as we'll see, is much more a function of the "bigger picture" or "larger system." As the larger system impacts the people within, their individual brains automatically and continuously guess how to respond to this environment without them even knowing their brains are "running the show" according to its guesses. Their behaviors, rational to them even if they appear irrational to others, are *continuously shaped by the interaction of their prior history and real-time interaction with others.*

- I believe that people, as the possessors of incredibly complex brains designed to maximize body budget efficiency, are *far more complicated than they seem.* This is not scary or annoying, but interesting and refreshing (although I clearly understand why your brain might not want to be bothered with expending the energy to figure out others).

WHERE DID ALL THIS COME FROM?

I'm a helper by nature, and always on some type of quest for additional knowledge.

I've spent my professional life seeking a deeper understanding of why humans do what we do, particularly when we operate in groups. This led me to a PhD in Political Science, advanced training in Organizational Behavior, and fascinating professional experiences in the military, political, and business worlds.

I am constantly seeking new information to support my clients, and I've been surprised by how often practitioners repeat knowledge that is out of date and no longer accurate (or was never accurate).

This book differentiates me and my work from other approaches. It is my stake in the ground.

My clients have found my work to be very effective in helping them understand the often confusing and irrational human behavior that occurs inside organizations. It is thoroughly grounded in updated neuroscience and solidly established theories on the functioning of humans with others.

A convenient label for the work I do is Executive Coach. If you look me up on LinkedIn, that's how you would see my work presented.

I've had the opportunity to work with thousands of senior executives and the C-Suite in professions as diverse as law, audit/accounting, banking, manufacturing, defense, design, construction, food/beverage, media/entertainment, health care, academia, government, and the nonprofit sectors.

But I'm far more than that.

I bring a unique, interdisciplinary background to the *art* of supporting the most talented executives in the most demanding fields.

I think this work should also be fun. Let's diverge a bit.

When I was young, I loved the film *Weird Science*.

The fantasy operates thusly: two nerds/outcasts create (via computer) what is essentially a life coach, Lisa. She is brilliant, funny, kind, and also happens to be gorgeous. In true teen movie fashion, Lisa helps the nerds gain some confidence, throw an awesome party, overcome bullies, get the cool clothes and Ferrari, and, ultimately, get the girl.

What she really does is show them that *they had it in themselves all along.*

My achievements in high-stakes environments—US Naval Academy, Fulbright, PhD, work on Capitol Hill and other halls of power, and with clients in top businesses and organizations—have served as excellent prep to support clients in a similar way as Lisa (modifying her blueprint for my own individuality, of course).

I, too, help my clients get what they want, through seeing *they had it in themselves all along.*

I feel I have won the jackpot because I get to do this work. I have a front seat to my clients' experiences, both challenges and triumphs. The more I spend time with them, the more convinced I am that their individuality is their best asset and the key to achieving their goals, if not their dreams.

Their individuality is also the key to everyone being successful around them. As you'll see, it's crucial for truly effective collaboration and teamwork.

The research and approaches I share have improved people's lives, and not just their work lives, but their personal lives as well. It's excellent research, based on the real experience of people.

Since executive coaching assignments are typically reserved for a very small percentage of individuals in elite organizations, I didn't want only those lucky few to benefit from this approach. I wanted you to benefit too, along with the organizations you work for and the people you are around.

Your presence matters. You need to be your best so others can be their best. Lisa knew it, and I'm sharing the research and stories that demonstrate it.

PUTTING IT ALL TOGETHER

Coaching is a tricky profession. Coaches work to deliver the organization's desired results (often a request to change a person in some way) to the sponsor, while operating in the tricky reality that basically no human can really change another human (Lerner 2014).

I've spent a long time thinking about this near-impossible task I'm asked to perform, and how to do it anyhow. It's one thing the acrobat and I have in common: we walk the high wire every day!

I've applied my own creativity, deciding the best way to approach this task is turning it *inside out*. That is, I seek to understand the organizations I support through the people I coach.

After all, we'll see that the performance of executives within an organization is less representative of w*ho they are as individuals*, and highly representative of the overall functioning of the organization itself. They are the proverbial canaries in the coal mine.

I observe this dynamic and help them see it too. When the canaries see what's happening around them, they nearly always figure out for themselves the right way to manage the situation to excel and get what they want. I serve as their partner along the way, drawing out their genius.

As an academic, I've applied top research to support my clients' genius. As a practitioner, it's awesome to see how applying this knowledge to their lives has enabled my clients to get what they want.

As a human who also wants to keep improving, I've been astonished how applying these concepts to my own life has also produced some amazing outcomes. It's made life more fun too.

This book is a result of what I've learned so far. From this point forward, leotards are optional.

ILLUSIONS TO GET US THROUGH THE DAY

———

Do you know what a magician's best friend is?

A drunk audience.

It's one thing to be talented at illusions and magic. It's another thing to have an audience whose guard is down, whose faculties are dimmed, and who are a lot looser and more open-minded than they were at 9 a.m. that day.

Here's the thing, however. A magician doesn't necessarily *need* their audience to have an impaired brain.

Our brains already do a good enough job of not doing a very good job. At least when it comes to interpreting our environment and what is going on with others.

We are all too ready to jump to conclusions. Some think we are *reactive*, but it goes deeper than that. Our brains are wired to *predict*—and we base our predictions on *guesses.* You know what that means. We assume.

You know what they say about people who assume, right?

Daniel Kahneman and Amos Tversky won the Nobel Prize in 2002 for their work on our brain's cognitive biases and failures in logic. Through their research, we have gained an incredible understanding of the flaws in our decision-making process—including our tendency to decide based on intuition and assessments that are flat-out wrong, and not statistically based or grounded in common sense—all laid out in Kahneman's magnum opus, *Thinking, Fast and Slow,* in 2011.

Behavioral economist Dan Ariely has written influential books (including *Predictably Irrational* in 2009) and given widely watched TED talks on the irrational decision-making behavior of human beings.

Academics and Leadership Practitioners Robert Kegan and Lisa Laskow Lahey have gifted the world with the concept of humankind's deep-seated *immunity to change* in their 2009 publication of the same name. They have spent years exploring how flawed individual beliefs and unhelpful mindsets have prevented humans from making essential changes, even to save their own lives.

Psychologists Maria Konnikova (*The Biggest Bluff,* 2020) and Annie Duke (*Thinking in Bets,* 2018) have also contributed incredible work to the field of human irrationality. Their work has incorporated first-person accounts of overcoming thinking obstacles to win poker tournaments, producing solid research on our brain's illusions along the way. In keeping with the theme, Konnikova wrote the chilling *Confidence Game* (2016) detailing how "con men" and other hucksters use our brains against us when pursuing and taking advantage of everyday marks.

These books have become bestsellers and must-reads, championed as the top work in their fields. They have been excerpted and shared in the most influential magazines and news outlets in the world.

It's fair to say that a lot of people have read their work and absorbed it.

But have they really?

It's not my regular experience that I'm working with a leader (someone highly likely to be at least familiar with this work) and they'll say, confidently, "I think (x) about (y) person, *but well, you know human brains being what they are, I could be wrong.*"

This literally never happens.

Most of us know we could be wrong with our initial assessment or even conclusion about others or situations. But it never stops us, does it?

I'm fascinated by this. My work as an observer of human behavior exposes me quite a bit to errors in thinking, both mine and others.

What does this have to do with teams?

Everything.

As we'll soon see, when our brain makes automatic guesses about ourselves and other people, we become the proverbial butterfly whose presence, thoughts, and behaviors impact the entire relationship network around us.

That includes our teams. It includes everyone.

It seems quite important that we start with our brains, understanding a little more about what is going on under the hood in each one of us.

THE BRAIN AS PREDICTION CENTRAL

For years, I've been a voracious reader of brain science and its intersection with human psychology. I've searched for scientific evidence on the connection between our brain's messages and our behavior with others.

I was thrilled to discover the incredible work of neuroscientist Dr. Lisa Feldman Barrett (2017 & 2020). Dr. Barrett's magnificently descriptive writings and engaging TED talks have significantly influenced and enhanced my own thinking, and even the way I live my life.

Since I'm not a neuroscientist, I must rely on the first-hand work of impressive scholars like her. The neuroscience presented below is a result of her research. I've used some of her terminology and wonderful, evocative turns of phases, while adding my own interpretations. For more information, I highly recommend her books and materials.

One of the more incredible and memorable points that Dr. Barrett (2020) makes about the brain is that it is *not for thinking.*

Rather, your brain's core function is to serve as master coordinator of your body, maintaining a strict budget of acceptable energy expenditures. Barrett calls this the "body budget."

This budget tracks the intake of core resources you need for survival (water, salt, and glucose). As I mentioned in the intro, when you "spend" resources on any activity, whether physical movement, inside-the-head thinking, decision making, or dealing with others, you withdraw from your constantly monitored body budget bank account. When you "accumulate" resources through eating or resting, you deposit into your account.

This is called *allostasis.*

Others contribute to your allostasis through their actions.

Think back to the last time someone gave you a warm hug. Or the last time someone insulted or criticized you. I'm guessing the hug felt tremendous, like a warm velvety blanket on a frosty Saturday afternoon. The insult or criticism probably felt like a punch in the face. You may have wanted to hurt the other person back. At the very least, it probably made you feel a bit off the rest of the day.

These impacts are not all in your head. They are felt throughout your body. The hug—sweet and caring—was like a deposit into your body budget. The insult or criticism, an overdraft in your bank account. We experience withdrawals and deposits we never asked for all the time.

Furthermore, allostasis isn't a "rational" process; it's based on guesses, not logic. Every action you take or don't take is your brain *making a guess* as to whether it is worth it to spend or save resources. It's an entirely economic process.

Further distorting this process, our brains are like a miserly friend; they would prefer to anticipate and avoid body budget withdrawal surprises, and to stockpile resources to prepare for the uncertainty of the future.

In plain language, our brains are penny-wise and pound-foolish, and not just on the basis of real-time calculations of what is a good expenditure or not, but based on guess-based prediction of whether the energy expenditure is worth it. Human brains are energy conserving, and they don't base decisions on logic or rationality, but on guesses.

This approach to survival goes back millennia. It's safe to say this is well-ingrained at this point, even if it may not always serve us well in interactions with others.

OUR BRAIN "IS NOT FOR THINKING"

As human bodies surpassed other creatures in size and complexity, we developed a command center (our brains) to manage this process of guessing. Think of this like a business that adds complexity as it grows.

Running this corporation (our bodies) is your brain's most important job—not thinking. It's not emotion, not imagination, not building skyscrapers, or dreaming up the next big tech start-up or blockbuster film, or curing cancer.

The main function of your brain, and my brain too, is to guess how to respond to energy needs before they arise, which ultimately ensures our brains can run our sophisticated bodies well enough to pass along our genes to the next generation.

Cavemen and women relied on prior experiences to provide reliable information to support allostasis. They were keen to repeat or avoid actions if that choice worked well in the past.

Humans aren't alone in relying on past experiences to determine their course of action in the present. Even simple sea creatures make use of guess-based prediction to determine whether to move away from or toward something that could either be dangerous or provide sustenance.

As a result of this automatic process, Barrett (2020) notes that our daily existence as humans is a carefully-controlled hallucination that is constrained by the physical world in which we find ourselves in, but very much constructed by our brains. Our brains' constant hallucinations create our experiences and guide our actions.

Through guesses, our brains create meaning from all the sensory inputs it receives every millisecond.

Typically, we don't even realize this is happening.

We think we observe "reality" and then respond to what we are observing (the classic "stimulus-response") pattern. However, our brains are constructing our reality through its guesses about what is going on around us.

Here's a simple example from a recent interview with Barrett (Skipper 2020): think of a Major League Baseball hitter at home plate, anticipating a 90 mph pitch.

He doesn't have enough time to see the ball and then swing. Instead, his brain is automatically computing all the information his senses are taking in and is making a guess as to where the ball will be.

His brain conducts this automatic analysis based on the last time he was in this situation. Rather than responding to what is actually happening, his brain is making a guess based on what he sees, feels, hears, and experiences that enables him to respond appropriately to the ball.

His brain neurons are firing automatically, changing rapidly in response to the guesses he is automatically making about the situation at home plate.

It is only through this rapid, automatic process fueled by our brain's best guesses, that baseball is even possible.

Off the baseball diamond, this automatic process occurs in every other element of our lives, including our interaction with others.

Furthermore, this process doesn't happen in isolation. It occurs while we are constantly embedded with other people, in families, societies, organizations, groups, and teams.

MEET YOUR "AGITATED YODA"

Let's take a step back from brains for a moment to consider the environment in which human brains operate.

When we humans think about our lives, particularly our challenges and triumphs, we think in terms of stories. Over millennia, human stories and myths have a basic flow: the Hero's Journey. It forms the plot for movies, TV shows, and other cultural artifacts, and is also how we think of our own experiences (Cooke 2019).

The Hero's Journey starts when the protagonist faces an unexpected challenge or call to action. Typically, the hero resists (they are scared, annoyed, too busy, or just don't want to be bothered), but they succumb to the call eventually. Shortly after accepting their fate, the hero meets their mentor, the guide that will help them face the challenge.

This should start to seem familiar to you.

Together, the hero and mentor move through the multiple phases of this journey, including smaller tests (the warm-up challenges that are precursors to the big test to come) and meeting other allies and enemies along the way. They face their own reluctance and shortcomings. Ultimately, they face a defining challenge.

They are a hero, after all, so they are typically victorious. The experience then comes full circle for the hero. They are reluctant to return to the way things were before. After all, they are different now. They have gained special and powerful knowledge through the entire experience, leading them to a higher level of operating. Then the cycle begins anew.

I want to zero in on the meeting of the mentor part of the Hero's Journey. A classic example is when Luke Skywalker (the protagonist) meets Yoda (the mentor) in *The Empire Strikes Back*.

In Luke's case, Yoda was a mentor met externally. However, when we humans face our daily lives, we also have an internal mentor within our own brains. Let's call it *Agitated Yoda* (or, AY).

Agitated Yoda stems from your brain's primary function: ensuring survival through managing the body budget. It gets this name because it's trying to help you, serving as internal mentor through everything you face every day.

At the same time, it's miserly, remember? It's agitated that you need it. After all, calling on it is sucking up valuable body budget resources.

Agitated Yoda is not the most reliable mentor. It is, after all, informed via guesses.

Your internal mentor's response to everything is *attack or avoid* (Smith 2019). AY wants you to get through whatever you need it for as quickly as possible. Its focus is solely on your survival and conserving energy. It often advises you to throw all processes into overdrive to deal with the situation (to get back to conserving energy as quickly as possible) or to downplay or forget about the threat entirely.

Sure, there could be circumstances where AY's mentoring may be optimal. If you must act on instinct to get out of the way of a speeding car, it's there for you.

That is one scenario where Agitated Yoda excels. However, you probably know that attack or avoid instincts may be problematic in a complex world. There are many opportunities for AY to be wrong.

Especially if we don't see its automatic mentoring happening, or if we don't take a step back occasionally to try to determine where Agitated Yoda's automatic instincts come from, and whether they are properly calibrated for the environments and situations we find ourselves in.

All in the name of survival, Agitated Yoda's automatic mentoring may make us less flexible, less adaptable, more impacted by the AY-fueled responses/emotions of people around us, and more filled with anxious energy—and it may make it more difficult to be resilient when we face setbacks.

AGITATED YODA IS NOT THE TYPICAL EXPLANATION FOR THIS PROCESS,
AND THE OTHER EXPLANATION IS WRONG

Let's consider a typical workplace example of Agitated Yoda: Charlotte is a Vice President at a financial services company, and one of my treasured clients. She is an incredibly lovely human being: intelligent, insightful, organized, and a pro at relationship building. She is a subject matter expert in her field and has natural leadership skills to boot. (People genuinely want to follow her: be on her team, be a part of her initiatives/projects, or just be a part of her orbit at work.)

Charlotte, like every human, has an Agitated Yoda. It prompts her to Attack or Avoid.

Charlotte's boss is freaking out because of demands from the Board. He is in the throes of his own Agitated Yoda mentoring. He's being sarcastic and snippy, and raising his voice at Charlotte and her peers. At some point in his life, his own Agitated Yoda became convinced that this behavior helps with his own survival, and this guess is automatically driving his actions.

Fueled by this unhelpful mentoring, her boss demands Charlotte and her peers *do something* to fix the problem he faces.

Charlotte's own Agitated Yoda is sending her automatic (and in this case, unhelpful) mentoring to "help her" with this freak-out. It prompts her to start questioning herself and her well-established, real competence.

Charlotte's AY also prompts her to be irritated at her boss.

All this obscures her own thinking.

She can't see that her boss is operating as a function of his AY. He's part of the C-Suite. Surely he can control himself, right? It prompts her to blame him, but then, faced with the survival threat of his demands, screams that she must *do something* right away too.

Charlotte's AY doesn't care if the s*omething* is the right choice. It doesn't consider *rightness*. It cares for one thing: survival.

Further, because AY is so annoyed for being called into action, it prompts her to believe her first idea is the right one.

Her brain will hold onto that idea, and her AY will prompt her to defend it and call into question the character of any other person *who dares to question it*. In this case, that means her colleague, Difficult Dominic.

To help this process along, Charlotte's AY will also remind her of the times when Difficult Dominic was wrong and rude to her. It will prompt her to think he's trying to one-up her.

Charlotte's AY must manage survival threats from Difficult Dominic and her upset boss. Its mentoring pushes Charlotte into action, staying late to pursue her (not so completely thought out) idea in a blind attempt to fix the survival threat of a displeased boss.

Prompted by her AY, she feels the need to do whatever she can to please her boss and prove once and for all she knows what she is doing (and related, that Difficult Dominic knows absolutely nothing).

Never mind the fact that Charlotte has been effective for decades and doesn't need to prove herself.

She can think clearly and save the day if she can step back and realize that her AY has the wrong programming as far as how to handle this situation well. It has blinders on, and its all-encompassing urgency to deal with the survival threat makes her forget her real competence and value.

Further, if Charlotte had terrible relationships with her team members, if she didn't trust them or like them, the outcome might be even worse. If she saw them as less important than her, mere resources she has at her disposal versus independent human beings, her AY might also prompt her to make unreasonable demands on them as well.

This would activate their own AYs, continuing the process through many levels in the organization. Her team might be resentful, thinking she only sees them as tools in her quest to relieve her anxious energy, which appears to come from her boss, but is actually a function of her AY being at DEFCON 1!

What a mess, right?

You've probably heard a different explanation for this common experience. Let's put that to rest right now.

Typically, coaches tell their clients that their emotionally unintelligent freak-outs stem from primitive emotions arising from the less sophisticated parts of their brains. They reassure their clients that, while the primitive emotions can sometimes overrule the more rational parts of their brain, they can take control back.

They typically note that a freak-out or amygdala hijack was a person's "lizard brain" taking over temporarily. This stems from the myth of the triune brain.

The myth asserts that the human brain has three parts: a "lizard" section operating on autopilot, a limbic brain that relates to our emotions and memories, and finally, the more rational neocortex.

This may feel right, but it's incorrect.

As Barrett (2020) details, more recent neuroscience indicates that there is no ancient portion of the brain that prompts bad behavior, nor is there a rational part of the brain from which good behavior emanates. These brain activities may even occur in the same parts of the brain, further calling into question the accuracy of describing this process as a battle between different parts of the brain.

The triune brain myth persists despite evidence to the contrary. Luckily for us, new research on brain neurons—the building blocks of the brain—renders this myth dead on arrival.

A word on why this has traditionally been such an attractive theory: basically, it separates us from other animals. It also comes from Plato, so it's...sophisticated.

Do you like to get in intellectual fights with Plato?

Here's the thing. Every animal, even Charlotte's adorable kitten, has the same neurons that humans have in their supposedly more sophisticated brains.

Turns out, *all mammal brains have the same basic blueprint.* Scientists believe that reptile and other vertebrate brains are *also* built in the same manner.

Take that, Plato.

Human brains are more complex than other animals *because managing our more complex bodies requires them to be.*

In any animal, the brain will be as complex as it needs to be to run the body within which it operates. It's not a function of moral or any other superiority. As a product of evolution, each brain is programmed to develop according to the needs of the animal it's in.

This programming runs longer for brains in more complex bodies. Since human bodies are more complex, the process runs longer for humans than in other animals.

Other vertebrates have the *same exact neurons* that humans have in their neocortex, and if their programming "ran long enough" their brain matter would eventually be organized in the same way.

This negates the scientific basis of seeing human brains as superior to other animals.

Here's the kicker: this work is so new that *many neuroscientists are not familiar with this research themselves,* and many others have only begun to update their beliefs accordingly.

RATIONALITY IS NOT WHAT WE THINK IT IS

The idea that we have an epic battle regularly occurring between rationality and emotion inside our brains is completely made up. We *have not* defeated our animal nature to rule over the rest of the planet.

Furthermore, *other animal brains are not necessarily inferior to humans*; rather, *they are adapted* to their specific environments.

In the popular TV show *How I Met Your Mother*, the petite character Lily, who grew up in Manhattan, teases her towering Midwestern husband, Marshall, about his gigantic size. She notes that, unlike Marshall, she grew to the proper size for her environment and then stopped growing.

We can think about human and animal brains essentially doing the same thing. Our brain size or its sections are not what makes humans awesome. They are merely a function of proper adaptation.

Nevertheless, since Plato, generations of scientists and philosophers have insisted that human brains are somehow different and special, and part of that specialness is our ability to "tame" our emotions.

Uninformed scientists, philosophers, and executive coaches all believe that, if we can just somehow control our emotions, our rationality will shine through.

It's just a simple matter of going to war with yourself. No biggie.

Unsurprisingly, this concept paved the way for *blame* of ourselves and others.

Generally, we believe it is immoral to let our irrational behavior rule our actions. We even judge and shun people who cannot or will not behave rationally (i.e., who seemingly aren't going to war with themselves to master their emotion/instinct).

Rational behavior is often described as thinking-based or behaving without emotion.

But is it irrational to have strong emotions or to feel fear when your life is threatened (or you just think strongly that your life is threatened)?

Furthermore, is all our thinking rational? Charlotte's response to her boss was based on her initial thinking. But it wasn't necessarily rational.

Barrett (2020) suggests that rationality might be better defined as saving or spending body budget resources to succeed in the immediate environment.

AY is rational when it comes to body budget threats. If you have a cortisol rush when encountering a threat, AY is being rational, ensuring our survival.

From a body budget perspective, AY operates rationally in all of these scenarios:

- Alarm in response to actual threat

- False alarm (no actual threat but the environment is threatening)
- False alarm (no actual threat and the environment is not threatening, i.e., PTSD)

It's still doing its best to keep us alive.

Let's take a step back for a moment and remove the value judgments and misunderstandings around rationality.

It really is the proper investment of our resources, regardless of the situation.

It is not irrational (from a body budget perspective) to have emotions.

Our AY is a function of our brain's prime directive for survival. When our brain's assessment of the situation is incorrect, the misinterpretation is not a defect in the brain itself. Still, to help our AY's predictions, we can update its assessment to ensure it fits in the current environment.

Not doing this is like not updating your computer or your phone. Eventually, these devices will not work properly anymore in their current environment or won't do what you need them to do for you.

AY automatically tries to protect us from survival threats, but we don't have to take its first prediction.

Like the baseball player in the earlier example, we cannot completely avoid an erroneous swing that resulted from our brain's best guess in the moment. Those are going to happen, and they are not a function of irrationality and they do not make us deserve blame. However, we can continue to update our brain's capacity to more accurately interpret the sense data from all around us to make better "guesses" and, ultimately, more effective responses to the people and environments around us.

WHERE DOES AGITATED YODA (AY) COME FROM ANYWAY?

In a beautiful turn of phrase, neuroscientist Lisa Feldman Barrett describes the human brain as a Master of Deception (2017) because our experiences, and therefore our emotions, are *actually created by our brains.*

You read that right.

Our brains constantly supply us with the *illusion* that external events *cause* our emotions.

However, our brains are so fast and are such masters of predictions based on prior experience that the process occurs this way: our brain makes its best guess based on the status of our body budget, which then leads to our emotions.

We don't perceive the guess because it happens so quickly. This default process (I call it default mode) is so automatic that we think the process starts with the External Cause.

More specifically, our brain guesses that the emotion starts with the External Cause. Then we accept that guess as truth because, well, this process happens so quickly that this is what it feels like in our brains.

Barrett (2017) suggests, and I agree, that we may want to rethink emotions and understand they stem from biology (AY's attempt to rationally manage the body budget).

Because our brains simplify things to conserve energy, we often end up with the wrong theory of mind: our brain's theory as to what is going on inside it, and why we feel these different emotions.

Let's review:

AY's rationality (its ability to manage the body budget) is only as good as its programming, which then impacts its guesses and automatic interpretation of what is happening around us.

As a result, *our emotions stem from our bodies, mediated through our brains.* This occurs through a rapid guess process.

We might want to reconsider the concept that someone else caused our emotions.

When AY interprets something as a threat, this is a product of evolution, our experiences, and how we receive, shape, and learn about our experiences. But it's just a guess.

THE CREATION OF WHAT WE EXPERIENCE AS REAL
You, me, and Charlotte experience social reality—what we think is real as constructed by all of us—as actual reality.

My brain, your brain, and everyone else's brain combine forces automatically to create the experience we perceive as real.

Before we could do it for ourselves, other people balanced our body budget for us. This impacts our response to others. Our brain neurons developing inside us were influenced by other people when we were young and very impressionable.

Our neurons continue to be impacted by others every day: other brains managing the body budgets of other people. Their brains appear to us through their actions, which shape our body budget and, therefore, our emotions. This continues to impact our response to others.

This experience has shaped not just the wiring in our brains, but also our *minds* (our awareness of our existence in the world around us).

Our minds come from our brain's incredible capacity to use *concepts* to predict and respond to what happens to us or what might happen to us. These concepts come from other people and our culture, and are necessary for survival in navigating our physical and social environments.

We use concepts as tools to appropriately manage the core dilemma of living with others: privileging ourselves versus privileging others. The core dilemma in teamwork.

Each of our brains were formed and impacted by the cultures and environments in which we have existed and continue to exist. This has not just formed our brains, but our minds. Yes, even our AYs.

This shaping occurs through a dynamic process called *plasticity*, where interconnections within the elements of our brain increase and decrease, including growing in completely new areas.

Our human experiences drive plasticity changes. Our experiences become encoded in our brain's wiring and change this wiring in the process.

Plasticity is how our prior experiences inform the interpretation of new ones. Hopefully, it also updates our AYs so they can manage the body budget as rationally as possible.

Billions of neurons inside our brains are constantly configuring and re-configuring themselves into different patterns, spurred on by neurotransmitter chemicals to construct events inside our heads. Human brains are complex, leading to their amazing ability to build new patterns through the combination of preexisting patterns.

For example, you can accept AY's default survival threat interpretation that your boss is upset with you personally, as Charlotte did, or you rework these patterns to create a new explanation in your brain.

Our billions of neurons are capable of being endlessly redirected to create an almost unlimited collection of experiences, perceptions, and behaviors. This is the truly amazing part of the brain, available to us thanks to our brain's ability to integrate all the information supporting our conscious existence.

Our brains became huge and complex to deal with our complex bodies. Our beautiful brains continue to create information and retain it. Finally, our brain cells provide us with multiple ways to interpret our surroundings, akin to having many different patterns of main and side streets to complete our commute.

We can create new options for AY's interpretation of our environments. We are the *architect of our experiences* (Barrett 2017), only limited by our body budget's constant demand for allostasis.

OUR BRAINS (AND OTHERS' BRAINS) CONSTRUCT OUR MINDS AND ITS REALITIES

Affective Realism, Concepts, and Social Reality are three core elements of our minds that are simultaneously created by our brains and others' brains. As you'll see, they impact AY's programming too.

AFFECTIVE REALISM

Charlotte is experiencing what she believes. In the heat of the moment, her AY (a function of her brain existing primarily to manage her body budget, and its automatic guesses) suggests to her that her boss does not trust her competence, which is seemingly a survival threat. This feels very real to her.

She doesn't know this threat is being manufactured in her brain. It feels like it is coming from outside. She then chooses a very real set of external actions in response to a threat her brain deems as real but probably isn't.

Recall that this isn't irrationality. Charlotte's AY is automatically (and rationally, from a pure survival perspective) responding via guesses gleaned from her prior experiences to better manage her body budget and ensure she survives.

The unique wiring in our brains lends itself to a distinctly human experience called *Affective Realism*. This experience is a function of Charlotte's brain's interoceptive network guessing at what is happening around her, as well as her sensory regions picking up on the predictions and providing her information supporting that her brain's guesses are true.

Although it is not irrational, logic and reason <u>do not</u> drive this process. Rather, the guesses of Charlotte's brain, along with her mood, drive her experiences and behavior.

In the heat of the moment, Charlotte is convinced that her boss is disappointed in her. Charlotte's brain conceptualizes her boss' emotional state. Her brain has constructed the belief that his mood is disappointed, which is a product of Charlotte's affect, a product of what is going on inside Charlotte's body.

Charlotte feels a threat and her AY is on it. It must be because her boss is disappointed in her, obviously!

The truth is, we don't know what's really going on in his head, including whether or how much her boss' mood is a result of Charlotte, or what she's done or hasn't done.

Even *he* doesn't know this accurately.

We cannot escape affective realism; it is a product of our brain wiring. We should tread cautiously in our interpretation of events and others' behavior, however, because our perceptions are like looking through a smeary windshield. They don't represent "reality" and leave a lot to interpret and misinterpret.

You can recognize affective realism when it shows up in the form of gut feelings or stories that we immediately believe or disbelieve. This phenomenon explains the appeal of learning things we already believe to be true, and how information that contradicts our established beliefs lacks appeal.

It also explains why we keep believing something even when the evidence doesn't exist, like Charlotte believing that her boss is disappointed in her despite the concrete evidence to the contrary. It leads us to be inflexible and feel that we are certain, and often sets up dramatic conflicts.

Affective realism is a function of our brain's body budget balancing. You got it: it's part of our AY.

As we'll see throughout the book, one of the only "cures" for affective realism and the distortions it creates in our minds is curiosity about ourselves, our experiences, our guesses, and other people.

CONCEPTS

Another essential element for survival created by our brains is our formation of *concepts*. These are created by our brain neurons influencing each other and being influenced by our interactions with others.

This process impacts and regulates our body budgets and the body budgets of others.

Think about a conversation with another person. While you are chatting, both of your brains are guessing and responding to each other. The movements of one person influence the sensory input and predictions of the other person. Our brains are being *rewired* through the messages we receive from our conversational partner, and we are rewiring their brains as well.

Our experiences as humans are constructed by our actions. We impact our environments and other people, and other people impact us.

We can experience a lovely, warm reciprocity when this exchange is trusting and affectionate. We can also be negatively impacted when this reciprocity is not. It can re-wire our brain in an unhelpful manner. As Barrett (2017) notes, we are *electricians* of our experiences, not just architects.

Concepts help us get along as humans but, just as with affective realism, they may be inaccurate. They may make us see things that do not exist, like how Charlotte sees her boss being disappointed with her. They may also prevent us from seeing things that do exist, like Difficult Dominic and how he may be an incredible resource for Charlotte in this situation.

Concepts limit our capacity to explore other possibilities. Charlotte's brain has conceptualized Dominic as difficult. He is far more complicated than this conceptualization. Her concepts may categorize him quickly, leading Charlotte to miss out on the potential usefulness of seeing him more clearly.

SOCIAL REALITY
Finally, our brains inevitably impact our mind through the construction of *Social Reality*.

When Charlotte was an infant, she depended on others to regulate her body budget because she wasn't yet capable of accomplishing this task herself.

Charlotte didn't yet have a fully functioning AY, so she needed her mom and others to provide for and regulate her body budget needs.

As they did this, Charlotte's brain created concepts based on her experience and began wiring itself for her specific environment, her social reality. Her family's social reality was structured by other people in their environment in a specific way. Since Charlotte was so impressionable and vulnerable, her initial social reality became real to her through her early experiences.

The fact that humans can create social reality through the communication of concepts *amongst our fellow humans* is truly amazing. Our *social realities* are wondrously diverse and full of potential, with only our physical reality and created cultural rules limiting us.

Our shared social realities have enabled us to create civilizations and concepts—money, laws, etc.—that keep society running smoothly because we all agree on their definition. These concepts seem very real to us, as they are such a core element of our day-to-day experience. However, we might benefit from occasionally questioning the basis of these concepts, given that they are created by other humans (with agendas).

A fish doesn't notice the water it exists within, and we typically do not stop to consider how the environments we exist in (both our built environment, and our social systems and concepts) have all been created by humans. We tend to accept this created reality as "real." Not all concepts are equally accurate and useful, however (for example, race is a social concept based purely on the amount of melanin in human skin). When we forget that we create this reality, we minimize our power to *update our beliefs.*

We can only wield a superpower if we know we have it!

ILLUSIONS TO GET US THROUGH THE DAY

In practical terms, we have more reasons than ever to be skeptical of our automatic responses to any person or experience. Our experiences are not reality.

Our brains are influenced by others. This then creates a mind which tends to misunderstand itself and what is actually going on inside the brain that has created it (Barrett 2017).

The certainty we feel about ourselves, other people, and the world at large is actually—based on the brain science— an illusion. As Barrett notes, this illusion exists to get us through our day (2017).

Thinking back to the opening, I'm not sure magicians need a drunk audience in the first place. Our brains are doing a pretty good job, without alcohol, of creating all kinds of illusions and inaccurate explanations for what is going on inside us and other people.

We've examined under the hood of our brains. Now it's time to explore a little more how other people are incredibly influential in the construction of our AYs.

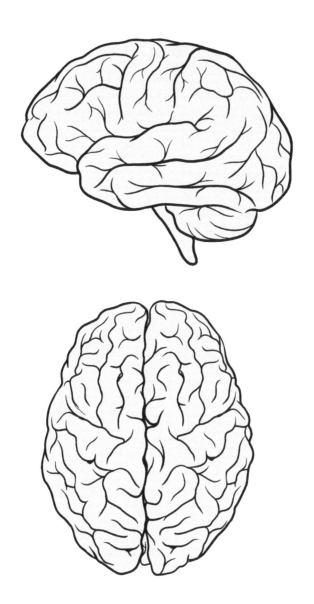

THINKING IN NETWORKS

———

I remember the first time I visited a therapist. I was looking for assistance in gaining further independence from family relationships. Specifically, I noted a pattern of behavior where I expected my family to be there for me emotionally whenever I had a minor mishap.

The catalyst was my twin brother saying to me, "I kind of dread answering the phone when I see your name pop up on my caller ID, because I know you only call me when you are upset about something."

Damn.

He said it in a kind but direct manner; it was stunning, but what he said was true.

I had just turned thirty, recently earned a PhD, and was in a stable relationship with my now-husband. It seemed like I had it all together. But clearly this was not how I wanted to operate in my relationships in the long term. I wanted to appreciate my partner and loved ones outside of them being my dumping grounds. After all, that seemed like kind of a jerk thing to do to people I truly respect and love.

Long story short, this is what led me to talk to a professional. She set a process in motion for me to start thinking a little bit more about the impact I had on people.

Up until that point, I had a vending machine view of love and respect. Like feeding dollars into a machine to get a Diet Coke, I was under the misguided impression that I could make people care for me and want to be around me because of what I'd accomplished.

Accomplishments in, affection out. Rinse and repeat.

I thought that was what they wanted from me, and I was determined to rack up these achievements.

Like in Skeeball, I wanted to keep seeing those tickets accumulating on the floor around me as I inevitably rolled more and more forty and fifty score pockets.

But similar to Skeeball, I had accumulated armfuls of tickets, wanting to trade them in for a problem-free lifetime of love and respect. I only ended up with the relationship quality equivalent of a few random cartoon character erasers and a small generic teddy bear.

I didn't want to keep living like this—hence, the therapist. In just a few sessions, she started me on a course to reconsidering my transactional view of close relationships and why I thought accomplishments were the key to love from others (the love of close family members and even romantic love).

I began to see that superb relationships are not a function of proving myself or my worth through accomplishments, and then making demands on others (in this case, to be my emotional trash can) in return. Rather, they naturally stem from being genuinely curious and caring, and knowing my own worth so I can be comfortable receiving love from others. Not in the form of a transaction, but more in the form of nurturing my relationships on a regular basis like one nurtures a houseplant.

Commonly, in families, romantic relationships, and friendships, we expect others to constantly be there for us so we can share all our biggest problems and anxieties, as if that is all they exist for.

Oddly enough, we think of those closest to us as the most important people in our lives, yet we openly joke about how we treat them in ways we wouldn't dream of treating others.

This has become a punchline in our society: that our family is forced to be subjected to our ugly sides.

Imagine the implications for the many workplaces that see themselves as "families." Is this just opening the door for people to treat each other in a not-so-nice manner? I think it's possible!

At any rate, my brain's best guess for how to off-load the negativity in my life was to dump it on others, and that didn't come from nowhere. My AY was wired this way at some point.

Somewhere along the way, my brain and the brains of other people (since this *isn't* a rare occurrence in our society) distorted that concept of "your family is there for you" into a less helpful thought pattern akin to "since family is there for me no matter what, I can dump as much crap on them as possible."

Recall how affective realism distorts our thinking, and how social reality and concepts stem from our culture and our earliest life experiences, when our lush brain tissue is extremely receptive to new wiring to construct our realities?

I share this story because of what I didn't want to talk about with that therapist: my family. Even though the issue I faced was prompted by my twin brother, I didn't want to delve too deeply into my family history with her. I thought it was super lame, unsophisticated, and frankly, blaming, to fixate on my family as the source of my problems. That was just so passé, eyeroll-worthy, predictable.

But I've learned over the years, in all my reading and research, that we can't just forget our families. We cannot understand our patterns around other people—yes, even at work—if we don't see where they were forged.

Our families are the first people we are exposed to. They literally and figuratively form our worlds. This includes the illusions and distortions that all brains produce when they make guesses to manage the body budget. Like it or not, they form Agitated Yoda in Charlotte, in me, and in everyone else, including you.

They are vital.

But don't worry. This isn't a book about your family, and it isn't a book about blaming your family for your work relationships. This is *not* a book about blame.

Blame is lame. Blame is lazy, intellectually un-curious, unscientific, and inaccurate. Blame is boring.

We *are* going to explore how people in our lives shape us, and how we shape them. For each of us, this process started with our families, and then continued with all our life experiences.

Remember, even right now our experiences and interactions with other people continue to shape our brains and our guesses, and we continue to shape theirs.

What follows is a matter-of-fact exploration of the sources of our brain's guesswork about the other people in our lives. It explores the underpinnings of these guesses, which create our default way of seeing ourselves and other people.

This default mode and our AYs came from somewhere! That somewhere is our earliest (and even current) experiences.

This is also a matter-of-fact explanation about how this default mode leads to warped perceptions about us and others, and how these warped perceptions directly impact the brain wiring, guesses, and, ultimately, behavior of other people.

To begin understanding this, we need to delve into a little theory first.

FAMILY AND ORGANIZATION AS BASIC UNIT OF HUMAN EMOTIONAL FUNCTIONING

For years I've been reading about Bowen Family Systems Theory and have found this theory to be incredibly valuable to my work supporting clients in organizations. This includes work by Murray Bowen himself (1982), along with Roberta Gilbert (2006), (2021), Kathleen Smith (2019), Michael Kerr (2019), Katherine Kott (2014), Harriett Lerner (2014 and all of her other books), Kathleen Kerr (1982), Ruth Sobel (1982), Kathleen Wiseman (1982), and the exceptional work of Jeffrey Miller (2019).

The work of Dr. Roberta Gilbert (2006 & 2021) and Jeffrey Miller (2019) have considerably influenced the following section. I am grateful for their clear writing and excellent conceptualizations of these ideas.

Now, let's get started:

The default approach to examining people's behavior is the proverbial person on a couch. They share their experiences, and then they and their therapist parse out these discussions for subjective meaning.

However, this process isn't very scientific. As you already know, we are unreliable narrators of our own experiences.

Enter psychiatrist Dr. Murray Bowen, who believed it was possible to remove some of the subjectivity from this process by understanding humans within larger networks—first families, and then organizations. This would make the study of human behavior more objective and more like other sciences.

His approach is like looking at a group of cells in our bodies and considering how they operate separately and together. This is more scientific than considering one cell in isolation.

He began his work with the study of schizophrenics, hoping to find a different way of approaching the most challenging problems of human behavior.

He believed, and was proven right, that his study of those with severe mental illness could eventually be applied to the less extreme and more common mental dysfunction more readily present in the broader population (i.e., our anxiety on a random Monday).

Dr. Bowen posited that any group of individuals who spend a significant amount of time together is *an emotional network*.

Charlotte, her boss, Difficult Dominic, everyone else on her team, and even their organization are in an emotional network. To understand even one person's behavior, we need to observe the wider network.

You may bristle at the thought of your workplace being an *emotional network*. However, that's why we spent so much time on the brain science in the previous chapter.

You have a brain. Your brain makes guesses about yourself in relation to other people so quickly you don't even notice it.

Your thinking explanations for this process surface *after the fact*, but your actual behavior and emotional state came from your *guesses*, which are *driven by your body*.

Charlotte's AY guesses, and this drives her emotions and behavior. As a result, she operates under the influence of her emotions at work, and so does everyone else around her. Furthermore, her AY's guesses are rational to the extent they help her manage her body budget.

Same for you, same for me. Everyone operates under the same influences, and we are all simultaneously affecting each other. These influences are drawn from our past experiences and our current experiences.

As I alluded to in the introduction, when someone acts in a dysfunctional manner, we typically label them as the problem (i.e., "Difficult Dominic is the problem") or the cause of dysfunction in the relationship (i.e., "Difficult Dominic is the problem between Charlotte and her boss").

Bowen theory suggests that Dominic's Difficult-ness stems from patterns in the entire network. We all impact each other within our emotional networks. Each person—operating in default mode and under their AY (without realizing it)—contributes their part.

We all influence each other without even knowing it.

PATTERNS IN EMOTIONAL NETWORKS

Early on, Dr. Bowen noticed that relationship patterns were challenging to sort out. In many cases, individuals were intensely "emotionally fused" with one another (what I call "melded").

As a result, if one person in the network became emotionally intense, another person would react in a reciprocal manner. Think: one AY doing its best to manage a body budget impacting another AY also doing its best to manage a body budget.

What's more, these emotional interactions were constantly occurring.

These reciprocal patterns, and our ingrained guess-based, typical human responses to these patterns, were so strong that even Bowen and his fellow expert researchers found themselves being drawn into the emotional intensities between their research subjects.

The leaders of emotional networks (like Charlotte's boss) would respond to stressors based on the patterns in their families of origin. Upon further analysis, these patterns persisted *across multiple generation*s.

Charlotte's boss's stress response started a long time ago. Now it's impacting him, Charlotte, and everyone else in his emotional network.

For all of you who are voracious consumers of articles and books that purport to rid you of your anxiety, here's a kicker: our anxious energy, along with our typical stress responses, may have been passed down from previous generations!

The patterns established by our families and organizations many generations ago have contributed anxious energy that persists and may increase over time. Founders themselves set the tone for the anxious energy in an organization, and their behavior determines appropriate responses to stress.

Dysfunction in emotional networks, including organizations, is a symptom of anxious energy and unhelpful patterns, stemming from generations of relationships in the network.

Charlotte's boss's unhelpful way of responding to stress is not a problem of who he is, but a symptom of anxious energy.

His brain, like all human brains, is wired to be sensitive to and therefore *constantly predicting* how to cope with his environment. With all the anxious energy around him, he serves as a lightning rod. He is trying to cope with this anxious energy the best he can.

As we saw in the earlier example, his anxious energy will constantly seek an outlet, moving in constant motion from person to person and generation to generation without any resolution.

Our brains enable us to zoom out and create new interpretations of what is going on between people. Using Bowen theory as a guide, we see that every person in a network is involved in the anxious energy of that network, even if one person seems to be impacted by it far more than others.

THE POWER OF THE 10,000-FOOT VIEW

Seeing networks has a tremendous effect on practitioners and clients. When practitioners work on themselves and understand their patterned responses to anxious energy, they are better at helping their clients. They can stay out of the anxious energy of their client's networks. This gives them more clarity and perspectives on what is going on.

When *practitioners work on themselves,* their clients can think more clearly.

This clears the way for the *client* to create amazing solutions for their problems, with the space and clarity they gain from working with a coach. They can move towards their own resolutions of their issues, rather than seeking solutions from others.

The same holds true for *any person* in the relationship network, especially leaders.

Think about the implications for leadership: for Charlotte as a leader, for Charlotte's own boss, and the CEO.

If Charlotte can step outside of the default mode, this creates space for all these people, not to mention those who report to them and their teams, to be less fueled by anxious energy (and contribute less anxious energy to the relationship network).

Generations of Bowen practitioners have contributed data on their clients' functioning (and their own), to produce a rigorous and valid theory of human behavior in networks.

Many concepts are particularly relevant for practitioners in the organizational development space, including encouraging clients to think more broadly about relationships in their network, as this is essential in improving anyone's functioning in an emotional network.

Furthermore, it all starts with one person. If Charlotte can improve her functioning, the entire network benefits. By short-circuiting anxious energy transmission, she creates more space for everyone in the network to think outside of default mode.

After all, others' brains *guess and respond* through their own wiring, but this wiring is influenced by others.

THINKING IN NETWORKS

Charlotte is only a fragment of a process much larger than just her. We can't understand her without understanding her organization and team.

Seeing how all the people fit together to form a living organism—the emotional network—is the way to think about networks.

Given the way our brains are wired, our anxious energy automatically impacts those around us in what Bowen theory calls *triangles*.

When Charlotte's boss and Difficult Dominic experience a high amount of anxious energy in their relationship, they will seek to include a third person (Charlotte) to create an outlet for this energy. This forms a triangle.

Inevitably, Charlotte participates in the anxious energy of the triangle, creating a conduit for it to flow around the three members of the triangle.

Unless someone in the triangle can take a wider view of what's happening, they won't see they are participating in the triangle. They also can't see if they are on the inside (a favorable position in the triangle) or if they are on the outside (a troubled position in the triangle).

There are many, many triangles in Charlotte's organization; they may occur whenever more than two people come together in any environment. Anxious energy (neither inherently good or bad) flows around and throughout these triangles. Triangles can also become interlocking when sets of three people form complicated relationships with each other.

Being able to see triangles is a critical component to observing relationship networks. If Charlotte can see she is participating in a triangle, she may see relationship dynamics more clearly, and come to different, more thoughtful conclusions about her colleagues' behavior.

Remember how the brain has a huge amount of complexity, with many potential avenues for accomplishing tasks and interpreting information? Human networks are complex in the same manner. There is constant room for new data and interpretations.

Thinking in terms of networks enables us to see the anxious energy around us in all its complexity, AY automaticity, and instinctiveness.

No human can stay out of triangles in relationship networks. However, if we can take the view of a coach of a sports team, we may be able to see our own position as well as the positions of others on the team. We can see how individuals operate in triangles and operate more thoughtfully in these relationship patterns.

The more we view our behaviors and those of others from a slight distance, the more we start to see patterns emerge in our responses. We might even see a replication of patterns from our earliest human experiences. For example, Charlotte—the "fixer" in her family of origin—may automatically play this role in the workplace as well. She may try to somehow "fix" the relationship between her boss and Difficult Dominic.

We each have many relationships, and we bring our position in our early and most important relationships to other contexts, including our workplaces.

By cultivating curiosity for and attempting to understand how we and other people bring our positions in one relationship network (i.e., our families) to other contexts (i.e., our workplaces), we are more likely to have a less automatic and more accurate view of human behavior.

There is great value in understanding how individuals in relationships affect each other and how these relationships fit into triangles of larger networks.

CONSIDERING PROCESS IN NETWORKS

When we consider the entire network, we can observe the emotional transmission from person to person within it. By looking at the how, when, and "under what conditions who does what," we can gain a 10,000-foot view of how people posture themselves because of the anxious energy.

We may even note how anxious energy *changes* the relationship system in real time.

When Charlotte observes emotions moving through her relationship network, she can stay a little out of the process and retain more space for curiosity and clear thinking. This short-circuits the anxious energy in the network, providing more breathing room for everyone.

It takes a great bit of self-discipline for Charlotte to merely observe this emotional process between her and other people in her network. Based on her freaked-out AY, it's hard to not be automatically drawn in. After all, its default mode desire to fix things is still at play.

Her AY wants her to jump in and relieve her anxiety over other peoples' strong emotions. It wants her to quickly fix the perceived threat that other people are freaking out in the network!

Same with me! Recall how Bowen and his expert practitioners—because of their AYs—also unwittingly became involved in the anxious emotional networks of their clients.

I work on this every day. Some days are better than others.

I'll be honest: it feels like walking a tightrope to just sit back, observe, and <u>not</u> solve others' problems for them.

I can't emphasize this enough: the positive result of changing an entrenched, AY-informed pattern is worth the momentary discomfort of just sitting with my anxious energy about others' issues.

Can't hurt to try, right? You might like being less responsible for other people's AYs!

HOW NOT TO GIVE BLOOD WITHOUT REALIZING IT

What I learned from my therapist is that anxious energy, triangles, and what appears to be odd behavior in others comes from an interesting source: too much togetherness.

Not just in families, but in organizations too!

From the beginning of human existence, we have organized ourselves in families, groups, teams, tribes, and societies. We have also struggled with the paradox of maintaining our individuality while also maintaining a respected position in human networks.

There is an understandable pro-togetherness bias in human society because we believe so strongly that it is necessary for survival. It certainly is in our early lives!

This sets up our brain activities accordingly. AY is programmed to think that togetherness is necessary for survival. It guesses (and distorts) accordingly!

This persists throughout our lives. Every love song, every rom-com, every family-we-create-based sitcom celebrates togetherness. By contrast, individuality (i.e., Charlotte being the "truest Charlotte" she can be) does not have many cheerleaders.

People want us to be who they want us to be (the version of ourselves that is most convenient for them), not necessarily who we really are.

We struggle daily, even on an hour-by-hour basis, to achieve a balance that involves connection with others without completely losing ourselves.

Realistically, this balance is a tension-filled minefield. It alone is responsible for much of the difficulty we all experience in relationships.

The drive towards togetherness moves us towards others, spurring both the real and imagined needs of attachment, affiliation, approval, and validation.

This same process also sets us up to transfer anxious energy and selfhood to others. In human relationships, we regularly give up or gain self from others. Think of this trading of self as two people constantly giving each other blood transfusions.

Just like physical blood, which is necessary for survival, our brain interprets this back-and-forth trading of ourselves as *necessary for survival.*

As a result, we tend to trade self in default mode without realizing we're doing it.

When there is a large amount of trading self in relationships, the people in the relationship *meld* together, a process which takes two individuals and turns them into a singular, fused emotional network.

You may have heard of codependent relationships, where individuals have a "relationship addiction" to another person that includes a significant preoccupation with and dependence on the opinions, beliefs, and presence of another person (Selva 2021). This unhelpful relationship dynamic is also present in melded work relationships.

With melding, the individuals have a hard time differentiating themselves, or determining where one person ends and one person begins. They aren't just giving blood to the other person: they are like conjoined twins!

Anxious energy increases the togetherness drive, drawing people further together and creating a natural conduit for this anxious energy to move around relationship networks.

Within these networks, people may often give up (dump) their anxious energy onto others to feel better. This builds up their self, at least artificially. This is akin to what I was (unwittingly) doing with my twin brother.

Others take on this anxious energy (are dumped on) and feel worse. Being dumped on diminishes people's self. This process, which aims to achieve some type of balance in a relationship network, can become so automatic it results in permanent diminishing.

Neither person in this situation is to blame necessarily. Remember, anxious energy flows around networks. Anxious energy was being poured into me from other elements of my life, and my AY demanded that it find some type of outlet. AY convinced me that my brother was the right choice for this outlet. Its guess was wrong, however. I needed to take a step back (which I did) and build up more individuality as a bulwark against this anxious energy, to limit the amount being dumped on me, and to prevent it from being automatically dumped on others.

Overwhelming togetherness eventually makes people more anxious! They have lost themselves. They have given so much blood, they have become anemic; they are emotionally conjoined twins, so much so that they cannot think for themselves.

We came together to stave off threats. We experience extreme togetherness as melding, which supposedly soothes the anxious energy of being on our own, particularly in a threatening environment.

However, melding also produces dysfunctional behavior symptoms in people.

What can we do about this?

Individuality is an incredibly valuable antidote to the togetherness drive we are overwhelmed with in our families, organizations, and other parts of society.

It short-circuits the anxious energy flowing around networks of humans.

Individuals are people who can connect thoughtfully with others, remaining self-defined and differentiated. They do not automatically give or take blood from others. They stay out of the pressure to become a conjoined twin.

As a result, they are more functional—and more successful. This is obviously important for success in the workplace and teams.

INDIVIDUALITY REQUIRES AWARENESS OF DEFAULT MODE AND CONSTANT CALIBRATION

You know how people describe some things as "the dream?"

Well, the real dream is being able to balance our individuality with our desire (or the pressure we feel from others for) togetherness. This enables us to participate in and enjoy our relationships with others, without expecting others to complete us or be the receptacles for our anxious energy like I was expecting my twin brother to be.

I learned that too much togetherness produces relationship and behavior problems. We can dump on others, disconnect from them, or blame them. It can lead us to need attachment to or approval from others in an unhealthy way. We give ourselves up to obtain this attachment.

The more blood you give to someone else, the less you have for yourself.

Similarly, the more of your own individuality you give up (without even realizing it!) in an emotional network, the less energy and problem-solving capabilities you possess to reach for your own goals. You'll be perpetually anemic.

But we have the capability to choose differently from the default of togetherness even if AY doesn't like it.

Cooperation doesn't have to require individuals to give blood to be a part of the group. Instead, each person can be encouraged to be an individual, act responsibly for themselves, and contribute their unique talents and genius.

Thinking back to my opening example, I thought that, by racking up achievements, I was existing as the best one can be.

I now know my accomplishments were a manifestation of my anxious energy; I thought they were necessary to survive.

Meanwhile, the anxious energy building up inside of me from chasing external validation, instead of being an individual, would often spill over into my relationship with a loved one. I gave blood and then demanded it from others.

I've learned that existing as the best one can be is existing thoughtfully as an individual outside of my AY-determined default mode.

While not living for relationships, I try to participate in relationships and communication with others as a separate person who doesn't need to provide nor seek approval from others, who is open to others, and who views other people as equals.

We're always going to feel the pressure to give blood, and our AY may spur us to take blood from others as well. Freeing ourselves completely from anxious energy patterns and default responses is impossible.

But we can recognize these default patterns for what they are: automatic responses to anxious energy (which our AY translates into survival threats). Then, we can choose differently, outside of our automatically-determined patterns and according to our individuality.

We can all improve our relationship functioning—and our results—when we privilege our individuality while remaining in relationships with others.

We are all better, and we make others better, when—individually—we are the "I" in Team.

AT LEAST WE AREN'T "NAKED AND AFRAID"

As night falls the group gathers around the fire, marked by a circle of large flagstones, blazing red with heat. We hear the pulsing chirps of crickets in the background as firelight flickers across participants' faces. The island appears vacant except for this special ceremony.

The group has gathered to decide the fate of a man and a woman, and the mood is somber. Some sit, some stand, but all are placed in a dramatic backdrop of foreboding jungle greenery and tiki torches. Members of the group appear sunburnt. Their bodies are sinewy, faces sweaty, and their mien is exhausted. Beards are overgrown, and the women's hair is wavy and unkempt.

Now is not the time for vanity, but for a decision.

Who will be crowned the very first "survivor?"

We await the final pronouncement of Sue Hawk, the Midwestern truck driver and betrayed fourth-place finisher in the game. She's faced with a seemingly difficult choice of determining the winner: inappropriate and Machiavellian Richard, or her former friend and "Benedict Arnold," Kelly.

As a member of the dominant "Tagi Alliance," Sue enthusiastically participated in the systematic elimination of her competitors. Now, however, she is surprisingly bitter at having been (in her mind) betrayed by innocent-seeming Kelly.

In an impromptu and ultimately viral speech that would shape reality television for decades, Sue attacks former allies Richard and Kelly. In reference to the most prolific animals on the island, she compares the former to a rat and the latter to a snake. She informs all present of her "rat king'" preference, and goes on to detail—in grand dramatic fashion—her desire to punish Kelly for the betrayal.

As the final stab, Sue urges the jury to crown Richard as winner, believing they owe the "Island spirits" a finish as "Mother Nature" intended: for the snake to eat the rat. As a grand finale, Sue's vote singularly extinguishes Kelly's chances of a win.

The scene in this show, an early reality television lowlight, is not just unnecessarily dramatic, but exemplary of how easy it is for humans to get caught up in the anxious energy of their environments, with behavioral implications.

During her speech, Sue appeared to dislike Kelly with the heat of ten million blazing suns. She vowed she would never offer Kelly any kindness or assistance even to save her life.

Instead, Sue would let Kelly be eaten by vultures.

Sure, Kelly's actions precluded Sue from winning money and glory. However, the situation was *not* one of life or death. Despite the name of the show, there was no question that Sue would leave the show alive. CBS's expert medical team made sure of this, no matter how many literal rats or snakes the participants encountered.

Yet, Sue's momentary fury has been enshrined forever.

Moving from the jungle to the workplace: have you ever felt like Sue? Have you ever been under the influence of external threats, along with internal stress, and then lashed out—or been lashed out at by someone else? Has your AY prompted viral-level fury?

Have you ever lost sight of what was truly going on, with your emotions white hot like Sue's? Or have you been Kelly, who—stunned by Sue's speech—was de-selfed by Sue's anger?

Let's return to the neuroscience. Our brains *aren't* maximizers or optimizers. Our brains are the managers of our body budgets. *Guesses*, however incorrect they might be, are how our brains accomplish this Herculean task.

Recall that our brains aren't *guessing* in isolation, however.

Other brains have impacted us over generations and earlier in our lifetimes, when influential others formed our mental models about the world. These mental models continue to impact us through the way they influence how we *process and interpret* our day-to-day, minute-by-minute experiences, and through the patterns we all develop to deal with anxious energy and relationship stress, not to mention other threats.

This was happening with Sue in the moment. She may have felt "right." Her points may have felt "right" to others, who also ended up voting against Kelly.

Was it necessary for Sue to publicly savor the idea of Kelly's demise, especially a former friend, because she *may* have lost a couple grand?

Did Kelly do anything to Sue that Richard didn't also do? Why is it okay for him to be a snake, but Kelly can't be a rat?

Lest you think I'm blaming Sue, I'll lay it out here: she is operating as best as she can, given her very taxed body budget and AY. If anything, I have sympathy for Sue. Most of us don't have our most impassioned moments filmed and retrievable from the internet at any moment on demand.

Thank goodness.

Human bodies are complex. As a result, human brains are complex. That is a feature, not a bug. It makes human relationships more complicated than our miserly body-budget-balancing brain wants them to be.

As we've seen, this complication multiplies when groups of people come together under threatening conditions, forming teams that are necessary to achieve an outcome.

Survivor, now many dozens of seasons old, demonstrates this fact repeatedly.

Your workplace does too.

As *Survivor* also shows us, human interaction becomes exponentially more complicated under threatening conditions, activating all our *AYs* (which, remember, are only as good as their updates).

Let's look at the threats that organizations (and the people within them) face, so we can start to understand the underlying persistence of anxious energy that can impact team members' predictions and behavior, and ultimately how we perceive them.

THANOS, ELEPHANTS, AND NARCISSUS, OH MY

All organisms in natural systems have anxious energy at the ready to respond to predicted threats. Organizations, created by humans, are natural systems. As a result, organizations also experience anxious energy.

In and of itself, anxious energy is neither functional nor dysfunctional. It *happens.* However, it can become a chronic problem in organizations (Kott 2014).

Organizations respond to threats similarly to a human body. When there is a threat to any part of the body, the whole body's anxious energy increases. In an organization, every member will experience anxious energy when one member perceives a threat.

Whether it happens in an individual or a group, any increase in anxious energy drowns out clear, creative, and adaptive thinking as the default mode takes over and fills the brain with fear, illusory thinking, and reactionary decision-making.

As a note, my thinking and writing on organizational threats and the response of organizations to anxious energy are greatly informed by the work of Jeffrey A. Miller (2019), along with the excellent work of other Bowen researchers, theorists, and practitioners. I've used Miller's work to inform the following sections.

You are probably quite familiar with the types of *external threats* that organizations face. Not only are these threats typically obvious, but leaders may also be open to discussing these threats; there is not as much secrecy and hidden anxious energy surrounding them.

External threats (which we'll nickname as "Thanos threats" to capture their magnitude) can actually produce a rallying effect that can increase morale and direct energy and motivation.

Non-Exhaustive List of Thanos Threats:
- Global economic catastrophes (e.g., recessions)
- Manmade (e.g., terrorism) and natural disasters
- Changes in the industry
- Significant shortages of skilled workers
- PR disasters
- Shortages in raw materials and supply chain disruptions
- High energy and other costs
- Changing customer demand

- Regulatory pressures and hostile takeovers
- Unrelenting competitive pressures
- Demands from shareholders

Within organizations, we are often quite aware of the existence of these threats, and they shape both the long-range and day-to-day activities of organizations in a transparent way. To the extent that they can be addressed, organizations attempt to address them. Otherwise, they'll be toast.

The second type of threats (*Internal Unspoken*, or "Elephant," as in "the elephant in the room") are less obvious and less openly discussed. There could be great internal disagreement among leaders as to the real nature and extent of the threat.

Any discussion around these types of threats is fraught, as acknowledging the problem often threatens the togetherness of the organization.

Coaches and consultants may be brought into organizations to deal with Elephant threats. Sometimes, coaches are employed to change people's behavior when the issue is the threat itself. The unwelcome behavior may be a symptom of the underlying threat.

Non-Exhaustive List of Elephant Threats:
- Reorganizations and layoffs
- Management and ownership changes
- Underinvestment in technology and other necessary capital expenditures
- Inability to comprehend and change direction to meet new client/customer demands

- Unaddressed employee performance issues
- Adversarial relations between management and labor
- Conflict within families spilling over into family businesses
- The organization "talks out of two sides of its mouth," celebrating teamwork, collaboration, and togetherness while fostering cutthroat individual competition through performance management policies and incentives
- Goals and objectives are not clear to employees; they don't know what they should be doing
- Goals and objectives are clear but not realistic (i.e., not achievable in the current market conditions)

Organizations may deal with multiple Thanos and Elephant threats at the same time. Unsurprisingly, they will typically prioritize Thanos over the Elephants.

Elephant threats are too messy and complicated (and battling the internal Elephants does not engender the glory of overcoming external threats).

Internal threats typically do not create a sense of urgency for anyone to do anything about them. As a result, the chronic anxious energy that stems from these threats seeps into and poisons the interactions of the people within.

There is rarely wholehearted agreement about the nature of these Elephants. This disagreement causes people to take sides, which then precludes the necessary motivation and action required from the entire group to effectively deal with internal threats.

Helpful employees who identify and seek solutions for internal threats may sometimes provoke opposing factions or align themselves unwittingly with a faction. They may themselves be labeled as the threat. They certainly threaten togetherness!

Against this backdrop of external and internal unspoken threats, we identify one more source of threat: individual image threats (I call these "Narcissus" threats, after the famous Greek hunter obsessed with his own visage).

True to their nickname, Narcissus threats stem from our distorted survival fears.

Non-Exhaustive List of Narcissus Threats:
- Fear of being viewed as less competent or valuable, provoked by changes in technology or external market conditions
- Internal churn resulting from a strong need to be liked/accepted by people you manage or supervise
- Concerns about your performance (or your team's performance) vis-à-vis others
- Self-doubt and anger that you/your team are not sufficiently respected and resourced
- Pronounced fears that a subordinate's poor performance reflects badly on you (potentially accompanied by compulsions to spend more time managing your reputation rather than fixing the problem)
- Competition with peers for promotions and the pressure to treat them as rivals
- Fears that the company doesn't appreciate you, overworks you, or has otherwise benefited at your expense

- Feelings of helplessness stemming from responsibility for people or projects over which you have little authority
- Feelings of being left out when organization's vision/objectives change, undermining your sense of purpose and meaning (particularly if this new approach is not aligned to your preferences)

In an objective sense, Thanos and Elephant threats are serious risks to the ongoing sustainability and survival of the organization.

On their face, Narcissus threats are not.

However, anxious energy over *one* member's Narcissus threat is transmitted to the organization in the same rapid and powerful manner as anxious energy from the seemingly more serious threats.

Furthermore, Narcissus threats are rarely identified, articulated, and discussed, which makes them *insidiously* powerful.

No senior executive is going to come to a meeting with his peers and say, "Hey everyone, I can't deal with the anxiety that stems from the fact that I'm afraid you're all better than me. And on top of that, my team won't do what I want them to do."

But this anxious energy certainly shows up in the executive's presence and actions.

In some ways, this scenario is even less realistic when you consider the fact that the executive mentioned above probably doesn't want to admit to himself that he has these issues. He certainly can't see that his response to anxious energy is informed by generational patterns!

You can't deal with a threat that you can't see. You cannot address anxious energy that a person *is not capable of or interested in seeing* in themselves.

ENTER THE SURVIVAL SIX

Increases in anxious energy drown out clear, creative, and adaptive thinking. The default mode takes over in everyone. AY is calling the shots, and isn't particularly happy about it.

Anxious energy in and of itself is not the problem. What we do when we are in default mode can create the problem. We tend to do unhelpful things when we operate in default mode.

Our world is very complex, and the potential solutions to our problems are infinite.

Remember how affective realism, concepts, and social reality can impact, distort, and constrain our brains? The vastness of these infinite solutions is not accessible when we operate under the influence of our AYs. Our default mode solutions **may make things worse.**

We rarely experience anxious energy as something that is pleasant.

We typically want to *get rid* of anxious energy immediately. We often rapidly and automatically transfer it to another person. Organizations become a perpetual game of Hot Potato, and threats are not addressed appropriately.

All of us have dealt with anxious energy through these *postures*. They show how humans manage anxious energy. They are also *symptoms* of a high amount of anxious energy circulating throughout a relationship network.

These postures for dealing with anxious energy are not in and of themselves bad (although people tend to label them as dysfunctions). They are rational from an AY standpoint.

AY needs to get rid of the anxious energy somehow. This is how it does this in each one of us.

I call these postures the "Survival Six" and describe them as follows:

1. *Blame*: Identifying a problem person or problem department and fixating on their issues, rather than taking the time to consider what the "blamer" contributes to the situation, or how the wider picture/environment contributes.

2. *Conflict*: Participating in turf battles and other non-productive competition with other people or departments.

3. *Triangling*:
   - This is essentially taking sides with another person. "Person A" and "Person B" involve a third person ("Person C") after experiencing their "A-B" relationship as unsatisfying or unproductive.

- "Person C" may be who "Person A" vents to about "Person B," which shunts the latter into a lesser, outsider role in the triangle relationship.
- Sometimes, "Person A" and "Person B" agree that "Person C" is the problem, and they fixate on fixing "Person C" rather than the issue in their own relationship.
- This process balloons into a very complex scenario, creating a series of interlocking triangles, spreading anxious energy throughout the network, and forcing people to take sides.
- Participants (who are nearly always unaware of these underlying processes) may find themselves aligned with a specific person or group out of relationship loyalties or a misleading interpretation of the situation, rather than their careful analysis of what is really happening and an assessment of how they really think.

4. *Overfunctioning and (reciprocal) Underfunctioning:*
- One attempts to displace anxious energy or solve an incorrectly labeled problem by burying oneself in work, doing more than is necessary, over-performing and perfecting in tasks, or re-doing others' perfectly acceptable work products.
- This may enable the overfunctioner to avoid difficult or unsatisfying relationships with other people in their lives.
- Overfunctioning prompts a dysfunctional yet automatic reciprocal response in others: Like two people attempting to balance a seesaw, those around the overfunctioner will *underfunction.* They will do less than necessary, doubt themselves, and appear out to lunch in the face of the overwhelmingly strong anxious energy emanating from the overfunctioner.

- The underfunctioner gradually loses a sense of competence, self-worth, and individuality. As a result, they make mistakes. This realizes the overfunctioner's worst fears and justifies the continuance of this pattern. Both sides become burnt out because of this uneven interaction.

5. *Distance*:
- Distancing physically (increased time spent in the office away from other people, with the door closed; increased work from home; and increased business trips).
- Distancing emotionally (reduced communication between individuals or shallow communication where people don't say what they really think).
- Decreasing commitment to professional development and growth and severed ties to professional organizations.

6. *Cutoff*: The proverbial "jumping ship," where individuals will leave their jobs or career paths in the most dramatic distancing possible, trying desperately to finally be rid of anxious energy.

Organizational leaders may also constantly create and make plans to deploy dramatic and bold new initiatives ("peacocking") to deal with anxious energy, only to abandon these efforts without getting them off the ground.

They may also regularly provide mixed messages or instructions, policies, guidelines, and expectations that conflict with the official versions of the same. This unnecessarily complicates their employees' genuine efforts to do the right thing inside the organization.

LOGICAL STRUCTURE AND DEFAULT STRUCTURE

Charlotte's boss recognizes Survival Six behavior in his organization, but he has a plan for dealing with it. His organization is sophisticated; it has a *logical* structure that organizes its work, including organizational charts, policies, strategic plans, and official systems and procedures.

These represent how the organization is *supposed to work.*

He is going to use these systems and policies to prevent anxious energy in the system and rid the organization of dysfunctional behavior. These policies will keep everyone calm.

Right?

Imagine a remarkable situation in which his team has identified a Thanos threat, put together an exemplary and clear plan to deal with this threat through their best thinking as individuals, and has managed to not let Narcissus threats get the best of them in the process. This would be the proverbial "Blue Moon" scenario inside a workplace.

What could still get in their way? Charlotte's boss who, as a human, may officially prioritize one value over another in the *logical* structure, but who may not operate according to this prioritization in carrying out the team's plan because, under anxious energy, he actually prioritizes the values of the *default* structure instead.

Example: Charlotte's boss espouses quality above all else, including financial considerations, relationship considerations, or any other values. This emphasis on quality is widely circulated publicly in the company's marketing materials and is prioritized internally through a sophisticated *logical* structure of policies, checks and balances, and well-codified expectations.

Nonetheless, Charlotte's boss takes a routine meeting with the CEO, who has a favor to ask of him. He wants Charlotte's boss to pursue a relationship with a partner which clearly contradicts the logical structure priority of *quality*. Charlotte's boss responds to this pressure, his AY noting the CEO's displeasure as a true survival threat, and agrees.

He returns to Charlotte and her peers and directs them to operate accordingly. They can't help but notice that, despite all emphasis on quality inside the logical structure, what really appears important is the CEO's own personal wishes, regardless of what the company officially espouses in its logical system.

The CEO's wishes have become the de facto main value of the shadow system that determines how decisions are actually made inside the organization.

This is the default structure, named so because it is a product of the anxious energy default mode of the interactions, reactions, and relationships inside the organization.

When organizations do things that are outside of the official policies and framework of the logical structure, it is a result of the default structure.

By now, it's probably not a surprise to learn that the default structure is not inherently good or bad; it sets the tone for the culture of the organization and gives employees something to connect to. It creates the social realities of the people inside the organization, and interactions occur according to its demands.

However, when used to make big decisions, the disconnect between the default and logical structures is confusing (and AY-provoking) for Charlotte, her peers, and everyone else in the organization. The logical structure exists, but it is not driving the day-to-day operations of the company.

Facing this lack of clarity, people will just give up and start operating according to their own *default* modes. That is, not according to official procedures or structures, but whatever appears to work best for them in managing their body budget in the moment (i.e., whatever appears to quell their AYs).

***

Going back to Borneo, Sue, Richard, Kelly, and their allies set up a *logical* structure to support each other. Predictably, once the competition got fierce, that was abandoned in favor of behavior motivated by the game's *default* structure of "there can only be one winner."

Richard, the devious nudist, won.

Was it the best outcome? I'm not here to assess that.

What I do suggest, however, is that we start identifying the *threats* and *default* structures that operate in our organizations. How do they impact all of us? How do they impact our AYs?

In any network of people, everyone is connected to everyone else, and our brains wire the brains of those around us. As a result, anxious energy in one person circuits around this network, triggering the default structure (and everyone's AY), and impacting each person in the system.

As demonstrated, we can have incorrect guesses about the threats we face and can also have very unhelpful, yet patterned and predictable, responses to this circulating anxious energy.

These unhelpful patterned responses not only obscure the real threats and problems, but they create new ones.

TEAMWORK ISN'T SIMPLE, AND THAT IS TERRIFIC

———

"As difficult as it is to build a cohesive team, it is not complicated. In fact, keeping it simple is critical, whether you run the executive staff at a multinational company, a small department within a larger organization, or even if you are merely a member of a team that needs improvement" (Lencioni 2002, p. 185).

A lot of my clients have read Patrick Lencioni's *The Five Dysfunctions of a Team* (2002). Many executive coaches plan teambuilding sessions based on this book.

As you can tell by the opening quote, Lencioni is a fervent evangelist of the myth that teambuilding is not complicated. Furthermore, that teams will naturally spring forth from the green fertile earth like young mushrooms.

That is, if you quash the supposed enemy of team spirit everywhere: individuality.

Lencioni seems like a wonderful human with a strong moral compass and equally strong beliefs about the dangers of team members with independent identities (particularly women).

Independent men in the book are presented as somehow... less of a problem. Same with uncomplainingly compliant members of minority groups; they appear in the book as model team members. But they don't get the promotions.

I admire how aligned Lencioni is to the traditional corporate expectation that human behavior be reduced to the most simplistic, easy-to-manage, and digestible models.

This serves our addled body budgets and AYs' need for simplification. It just doesn't serve our *living in complicated times'* need for more sophisticated approaches to external and internal threats (and the behavior issues that show up because of anxious energy in the network).

When I first read his book, I wanted very much to agree with Mr. Lencioni. I wanted to believe that we can just take some personality tests, share our results, have some pizza at a nice resort, and magically be able to put our "egos" (actually, our AYs) aside to never again feel threatened by each other.

Then of course we can assemble like the Avengers and defeat the Thanos threats together (subsuming the AY provocations from Elephant and Narcissus threats to go after the "Real Enemy").

But as Richard, Kelly, and Sue demonstrated on *Survivor,* this is an illusion.

Importantly, however, they also showed us, with their ingenuity in the jungle, that the complexity of human beings is terrific. It's ability to spur innovation is our *greatest competitive advantage,* no tiki torches required.

That is, if you can get over your AY's protests of "it's too much work to understand the complicated nature of other people" to benefit from this awesomeness.

We first have to abandon our expectations that *The Avengers* is going to happen at our organization.

So, the bubble has burst. Lencioni's book doesn't jibe with the neuroscience presented earlier, nor the theories of human functioning in networks that have persisted and shown themselves to be valuable for decades.

It turns out, however, that Lencioni's fable is an excellent example of the AY-fueled point of view regarding teams that persist in organizations: *Why can't we all just get along? And why can't you just be and do what I want you to be and do so I can get some rest, gosh darn it?*

This point of view persists because it works for our AYs. It doesn't bring us closer to benefiting from each person's individuality. In fact, many practitioners and leaders believe individuality is the enemy and that it must be subsumed, rather than a valuable source of ingenuity, innovation, and clear problem-solving.

TROUBLE IN SILICON VALLEY: THE FABLE

The central premise of Lencioni's book is its presentation of his model of the "five dysfunctions": absence of trust, fear of conflict, lack of commitment, avoidance of accountability, and inattention to results.

Lencioni asserts that these five dysfunctions flourish when team members put their individual needs (what he terms ego, or their career development, recognition needs, success of their division) over the collective goals of the team.

Simply put, if team members care about these things rather than the collective goals of the group, the team will fail.

He explains his model via a fable he has written about a fictional tech start-up in Silicon Valley, DecisionTech. The fable surrounds a caretaker CEO re-creating an executive team after its CEO/Co-Founder was summarily removed from his job.

Overall, the book ends up being a terrific display of how threats impact the anxious energy of an organization and its leadership team, and how this anxious energy circulates around the people in the network. This drives them to meld, display Survival Six postures, and ultimately to not be at their best.

DecisionTech is presented as an overly political and unpleasant place to work. Its Board was jittery and unhappy with this negative reputation. Observers could not understand why one of the most promising, well-funded, and attention-grabbing start-up companies could harbor such dysfunction.

DecisionTech has an enviable *logical* structure, including an indestructible business plan, top-tier investors (including capital from the most cautious VC firms), talented engineers, and the most expensive and experienced executive team imaginable.

Thanos threats are right around the corner!

Operating under the unrelenting competitive pressures and demands from investors, DecisionTech has a lot of expectations to meet. It wasn't doing so well, however. The organization began experiencing significant issues, including the loss of critical team members, missed deadlines, and deteriorating morale. This was all despite its excellent position in the market and exemplary *logical* structure.

On the two-year anniversary of its founding, the Board unanimously fired Jeff, the company's thirty-seven-year-old CEO and co-founder. As consolation prize, Jeff was offered the job of heading business development and accepted the new position, not wanting to leave and miss his potential payout.

While some Boards may have been more patient with Jeff, DecisionTech's Board felt that the organization had too high a profile and too much at stake not to make a bold move. They were bound and determined not to sit idly by while the company "wasted away" due to "politics."

Employees expressed shock at Jeff's removal. They liked him. However, they didn't like the atmosphere of the company, which included no sense of camaraderie, significant backstabbing among the executive team, and sluggish and sloppy performance.

Now we have Thanos *and* Elephant threats!

The Board brought in a caretaker CEO, Kathryn. One of her first actions was to set up teambuilding off-sites to root out problems in The Staff (the derisive title that Kathryn gave to the executive team).

As you can imagine, all this upheaval and derision led to increased Narcissus threats in The Staff.

However, before we dive into a discussion of The Staff, let's review some of the threats that DecisionTech and its executive team faced, undoubtedly fueling significant anxious energy:

Non-Exhaustive List of DecisionTech's Thanos Threats:
- Unrelenting competitive pressures
- Demands from owners, investors, and shareholders
- Changes in the industry
- Significant shortages of skilled workers
- PR disasters

Non-Exhaustive List of DecisionTech's Elephant Threats
- Management and ownership changes
- Unaddressed employee performance issues
- Reorganizations and layoffs
- Goals and objectives are not clear to employees; they don't know what they should be doing

- Goals and objectives are clear but not realistic (i.e., not achievable in the current market conditions)
- Adversarial relations between management and labor
- The organization "talks out of two sides of its mouth," celebrating teamwork, collaboration, and togetherness while fostering cutthroat individual competition through performance management policies and incentives

Non-Exhaustive List of DecisionTech's Narcissus Threats:
- Jeff's management role appeared to conflict with his "nice guy" persona
- Jeff and others were overly preoccupied with concerns about DecisionTech's position in the market and whether his organization, his own performance, and that of his team were "good enough" as compared to others in the industry
- Many team members felt that they and their teams were not sufficiently respected and resourced
- There was a competition between The Staff regarding whether their teams are sufficiently respected and resourced vis-à-vis each other
- The Staff had unclear roles
- The Staff felt helpless over perceived responsibility for people and projects over which they had no official power or authority over
- The quick removal of Jeff and the appointment of Kathryn (an outsider whom the team was very skeptical of) was traumatic in and of itself; Kathryn's approach represented an extreme change from the vision and organizing principles under Jeff

- The Staff felt left out when Jeff was removed as CEO and Kathryn came in
- The Staff expressed fears that the company didn't appreciate them and their efforts, and that Decision-Tech was benefitting at their expense

DEFAULT MODE THINKING DRIVEN BY THANOS, ELEPHANTS, AND NARCISSUS

At first, team members appear relieved with the decision to fire and then re-hire Jeff for a more junior position. This aligns with what typically happens when an organization makes an extreme decision while operating in default mode.

People feel what they think is relief when their AYs prompt them to *do something*. This is especially true in an organization when a person who appears to be the initial source of problems and anxious energy is removed.

However, like a pesky leak, this anxious energy reappears in the system in other forms later. As the rest of the book indicates, the path forward for The Staff was not necessarily smooth, and there was quite a bit of human wreckage to come because of this decision.

Let's start with the anxious energy introduced into the system when the Board decided to fire Jeff and appoint Kathryn. Below are some clues that this wasn't a result of careful and clear thinking, but a true AY-fueled action from the Board, and the Chairman in particular:

- The Chairman chose Kathryn to replace Jeff as a function of his "good instincts about people." (Recall that "gut feelings" are a result of affective realism, not clear thinking.)

- The Chairman also had the same "good instincts" about Jeff, and he was wrong.

- Furthermore, the Chairman "reasoned" (which is code for pretending to access clear thinking while actually relying heavily on his anxious energy-driven AY) that "he wouldn't make the same mistake twice."

This was what the Chairman wanted to believe himself and have others believe along with him. It was wishful thinking dressed up in the psychological energy of a strong concept: "The Chairman's Wisdom Shouldn't Be Questioned."

Lest you think I'm being too hard on the Chairman, may I remind you, *he was wrong about Jeff.* That's okay. He is a human and allowed to be wrong. But it also suggests that maybe some further analysis is in order when he wants to push his AY's opinions about people on others.

Not for nothing, the Chairman was also responding through his AY when he fired Jeff. He didn't list logic-based reasons directly connected to Jeff's performance as the reasons behind his firing. He was operating under extreme stress and pressure (feeling that too much was at stake and the company had too high a profile to continue with Jeff at the helm).

However, there is zero evidence in the fable that Jeff was directly responsible for any of the vague issues (increasingly troubling atmosphere, backstabbing, no sense of unity, and things taking too long) that Lencioni lists as the problems with DecisionTech.

What's more, if Jeff was so toxic, why was he allowed to stay at the company and become its Director of Business Development?

While we're at it, the issues listed above seem like vague and ambiguous problems. Perhaps if the Board could have determined more *specific and objective* challenges at DecisionTech they could have logically and objectively assessed Jeff's role in the problems, rather than just making him a convenient person to blame.

Remember, blame is a sign of anxious energy.

A few other points that indicate how the Chairman was operating in default mode when he made the decision to appoint Kathryn:

- Board Members "questioned the Chairman's sanity" when he floated Kathryn's name as replacement CEO, but he "eventually wore them down." Wearing people down doesn't sound like calm, logical, non-anxious-energy thinking.

- DecisionTech was presented as being in a "desperate situation" and the Chairman insisted that there weren't too many capable executives willing to take on such a messy job, given the current situation at the scarred company. The presence of a desperate situation clearly impacted the Chairman's AY. He appears to be in an overfunctioning posture, forcing his perspective on the Board (who take an underfunctioning posture in response).

- The Chairman was determined to hire someone he knew and could trust. That is, the Chairman privileged someone with whom he had a *relationship* (a sign of togetherness pressure), rather than the objectively best person for the job.

Jeff's firing/lesser role and Kathryn's hiring is, on its own, evidence of significant anxious energy and AY-fueled decision-making present in the DecisionTech relationship system. In turn, this sets the stage for increased anxious energy and Survival Six behavior among the team members.

WHAT WAS REALLY THE PROBLEM WITH THIS TEAM?

Let's cut to the chase.

The book ends with a sample team assessment that readers can take to further understand the potential dysfunctions within their own teams. This assessment is very clearly aligned with Lencioni's point of view that the most damaging *threat* to a team is individuality.

Not Thanos threats. Not Elephant Threats. Not even Narcissus threats.

But individuality. That's the problem.

But individuality wasn't the enemy here. The real villain, so to speak, was a lack of anyone—not the Chairman nor the rest of the Board, not Kathryn, and not any of the team members—recognizing that an incredibly high amount of *anxious energy* was circulating around the network.

This anxious energy (and the inability of anyone to see it) prompted unhelpful guesses among the team members' AYs and provoked ultimately unhelpful, patterned (and selfish-appearing) ways of dealing with this anxious energy.

No one took a step back, took a breath, and tried to see things from a wider point of view. They didn't attempt to gain a level of clarity on what was really happening. This clarity would have enabled them to choose differently compared to our patterned ways of dealing with anxious energy: blaming and other Survival Six behaviors.

The Board, and especially the Chairman, didn't try to find out clearly what was going on within the organization before he impulsively replaced Jeff with Kathryn.

Kathryn, feeling the heat to prove herself, also didn't try to find out clearly what was going on. She didn't set up clear roles and expectations for her team members to bolster their logical structure and ensure it – and not the default structure – was followed consistently.

Kathryn's most important job as the leader of this team was to establish clarity in the logical structure within which each highly talented, intelligent, and respected individual could bring their full talents and full genius to their work without any unnecessary melding.

Yet Kathryn is also just a human being. Her need to prove herself, and the additional anxious energy that was introduced into the team by the sudden firing of Jeff, ratcheted up the threats on all the team members and obscured her own clear thinking.

Kathryn set out almost immediately to fix the relationships between members of The Staff through increased togetherness (actually, melding: where all the team members begin to think like her, or else be cast out). Kathryn, embodying Lencioni's core message, believes fervently that melding (stamping out any individuality) is the solution to the team's problems.

In Kathryn's mind, individuality is the threat, and togetherness is the solution. From the very beginning, Kathryn decries selfish individualism as the number one barrier to team cooperation.

To prove her ability to *do* something, Kathryn relies heavily on her AY to root out the problematic selfish individualists among The Staff. She demonstrates confirmation bias by looking for (and finding) reasons to stick with her initial positive or negative impressions of team members.

Undeniably, the pressure that Kathryn is under is intense. Her anxious energy impacts the performance of The Staff, bringing out example after example of their patterned, AY-driven Survival Six behaviors.

Much of the book is devoted to Kathryn's attempts to tame these Survival Six behaviors. She never realizes that her need to prove herself, along with her insistence in fostering melding in the relationship system, is fueling these selfish-appearing behaviors in the first place. This situation comes to a head through the performance of a highly talented yet very insecure team member, Mikey.

As the anxious energy in the relationship system increased, team members either quit or melded their thinking to Kathryn's point of view. Mikey resists and is shunned. The Staff begin to treat Kathryn's internal nemesis, Mikey, as an outcast.

In Kathryn's eyes, Mikey is selfish individualism in the flesh. Yet this is an illusion. Under the extreme pressure from Kathryn and unhelpful treatment by her peers, Mikey starts to show more intense Survival Six symptoms, giving others more "reasons" to shun her.

Yet Mikey is more like Kathryn than Kathryn probably would ever want to admit. They are both obsessed with proving themselves.

Both Kathryn and Mikey's behavior are being prompted by external and internal threats. Despite what Kathryn's AY guesses, Mikey's actions were not a sign of an overly large ego, but an overly sensitive and insecure AY.

Mikey's biggest problem was her AY's gaping, black hole need for validation from others, and her inability to perceive the anxious energy circulating around the relationship network as the catalyst aggravating that need. This was further spurred on by her AY's guess that her peers didn't respect her. The anxious energy from this thought pattern compelled her to act in problematic ways, setting her up to be the convenient object of blame when the team needed to make her its sacrificial offering to the "Gods of Relieving Some Anxious Energy."

Mikey was trying to prop herself up, to feed that black hole, but her actions were being interpreted by those around as enhancing her individual status.

What the characters in the book decry as politics (i.e., individual needs eclipsing the needs of the team) ends up being a group of insecure people responding through their AYs in the face of an overwhelming amount of Thanos, Elephant, and Narcissus Threats. Anxious energy repeatedly circulated around the DecisionTech team, spawned by the original sin (or in this case, original source of anxious energy): the outrageous and untenable "rock star" expectations of DecisionTech.

The team members, being incredibly experienced and intelligent themselves—even Kathryn begrudgingly labeled Mikey as a "brand genius"—attempted to cope as well as they could. But their attempts at coping with the constant circulation of anxious energy would often just provoke more anxious energy, and ultimately unhelpful responses, in their fellow team members.

Eventually something had to give, and that something was Mikey. She was the most vulnerable team member due to her lack of confidence in herself. Anxious energy settled into her, and what she thought was her best effort at coping (based on her brain's wiring) ended up getting her fired.

Kathryn, doing her best, attempted to deal with this anxious energy by engaging in what a lot of executives (and executive coaches) think is the answer: fostering *intense togetherness* among team members. However, Kathryn's team sessions just ended up causing her team to meld and their thinking to be dulled.

Faced with losing their individuality, the team member's AYs panicked; they were giving too much blood to DecisionTech to continue to survive. This increased their anxious energy further, bringing more into the relationship network and spurring more symptoms of the Survival Six within team members, particularly Mikey.

No one is to blame here, necessarily. Remember, blame is lame. Everyone is doing their best, trying to cope. Generally, they are following what they believe to be the finest strategy in dealing with all the expectations and anxious energy. Sometimes their AYs get the best of them.

The anxious energy isn't the problem. It just occurs. However, the team's less-than-helpful responses to the anxious energy led to further problems.

The real issue is that no one could see this process happening, and to choose a different way of thinking and acting in response to the overwhelming anxious energy circulating around them.

A THOROUGHLY MELDED DECISIONTECH

After Mikey is fired, The Staff become needier with each other and draw together, exhibiting further signs of melding.

This is predictable, as teams typically exhibit a melding response to a traumatic event. Kathryn interprets this as a "renewed collective purpose," but The Staff's postures following this dramatic climax have the classic hallmarks of an anxious energy response.

In turn, this anxious energy circulates from the leadership team to the rank and file throughout the company, who react negatively to the news of Mikey's firing. They express further discontent with the leadership team.

Interestingly, Kathryn does admit to the team that, earlier in her career, she was fired for failing to remove a poor performer. She reveals this information to increase their morale and legitimize her decision ("I did this to get the rest of you to stay"), but it serves as further evidence that Kathryn made the decision to fire Mikey because of her anxious AY.

DecisionTech ends up having some good quarters and some less-than-stellar quarters, like most organizations. Overall, the leadership team generally fails to deliver on its promise of being expensive, experienced rock stars.

They acquiesce to Kathryn's anxious overfunctioning posture, subsuming their individuality to follow her direction.

They clearly learned the lesson that Mikey's individuality was her undoing, and are determined not to repeat her mistake, lest they be the next victim of Kathryn's AY.

INDIVIDUALITY IS NOT THE ENEMY; TOGETHERNESS IS NOT THE ANTIDOTE

Teams get results when they have clarity, operate in a relatively non-anxious environment, and everyone (including the leader) gets the hell out of each other's way.

Overwhelming togetherness, leading to melding, *appears* to be the right approach in getting people to act collaboratively. Lencioni certainly believes this is the case.

After all, our brains are wired to think that togetherness is the default best practice when it comes to interacting with others, because our AYs believe fervently that togetherness is essential for survival.

But, as I established earlier, our behavior under the impact of too much togetherness ironically leads us to acting in ways (Survival Six) that prevent collaboration, promote groupthink, and ultimately damage relationships and results.

Togetherness can be lovely, don't get me wrong. But too much of it (melding), as we often expect and coerce out of people in the workplace, will create and magnify performance issues. Melding lends itself to anxious energy and *default* behavior. Lencioni's fable is rife with examples of unhelpful default behavior on the part of The Staff.

Melding doesn't lead to the clearest decision making, and it significantly impedes innovation. From a brain standpoint, it's like being on a candy high, and we might want to re-think the value of spending every day in such a fog.

Togetherness is not the antidote to team issues. Individuality is not the enemy, or the source of all team dysfunction. A focus on individual success is not a character flaw but a rational response to anxious energy, lack of clarity, and inconsistency in DecisionTech's competitive environment and its leadership (the Chairman, the rest of the Board, and Kathryn).

It's quite rational to think to oneself: "I don't know what I'm supposed to be doing, or what people really want or value around here, so I guess I'll do what I think I need to do to survive."

Ambiguity doesn't just make it easy to focus on individual success. Ambiguity breeds anxious energy, which people typically respond to through their AYs best guesses as to how to relieve themselves of the body budget threat of anxious energy. As we've established, the guesses our AYs make under the uncertainty of an organization operating in default mode will predictably make the problem worse.

Threats aren't going away. What can help is not more forced togetherness. That tends to bring on other problems. The answer is increased clarity in goals and performance expectations, consistency in leadership actions (particularly, leaders operating in accordance with the logic system rather the default system), and more breathing room for individuality.

Individuality is the key to getting people out of their default mode operating patterns. Individuality provides incredible strength and power to people attempting to resist groupthink, along with the default behaviors which make everyone else (and the system) more anxious in the long run.

Many consultants and coaches have decided that the only way organizations can overcome threats, solve their problems, and ensure success is by melding together, fusing to the point where individuality is suffocated in the name of the collective.

Running your organization as a family (isn't one enough?) or being hell-bent on subsuming individual identity in the name of the needs of "the Borg," doesn't just give us brain fog, it induces anxious energy.

I can understand why Lencioni wants to assure his readers that creating a cohesive team is simple. Just get rid of the individualists who appear threatening to our AYs. That fits our body budget needs just fine, doesn't it?

But it's not simple. Human beings aren't simple. While that may be annoying, it's also terrific. In a complex world with complex threats, it's our greatest superpower.

Like all organizations operating under tremendous pressure and expectations, DecisionTech needs more exemplary individuals like Mikey to bring their best work and selves to their team. Mikey's individual genius was the key to delivering DecisionTech out of their performance and innovation rut.

However, her true talents weren't recognized or appreciated in the midst of the anxious energy swirling around DecisionTech. Kathryn's message to the team was clear: conform to her AY's expectations or else. The pressure Kathryn put on the team to subsume their talents under her narrow prescription for togetherness and appropriate behavior (to solve Kathryn's own immediate need to prove herself) led to the loss of DecisionTech's star player.

This is what happens in organizations when they privilege togetherness over individuality.

INTERLUDE: INDIVIDUAL GENIUS

———

The Trevi fountain whooshes and splashes in the background, and the faint waft of espresso and acrid sweetness of cigarettes tickle your nostrils. Heat rises from cobblestones as you sit at your café table, listening to the high-pitched buzz of Vespas zooming down back alleys and slaloming through boulevards.

Faintly, you hear the familiar rise and fall of voices, passionately discussing a soap opera or politics. Ah, Roma! (Cue chef's kiss!) What a majestic place, full of history, religion, culture, superstition, politics, power, and beautiful Italian people!

Roma of modern day encompasses exceptional history and architecture, reminding all of us to this day of the impressive influence and persistence of its culture and ideas, and its contributions to language, architecture, and society, which persist even if modified for today's sensibilities.

Out of so many impressive contributions (and I admit it: as a proud Italian-American, I'm biased), one of the most beautiful concepts bequeathed from ancient Rome is the concept of "genius."

In this instance, I'm not referring to our modern-day TV and movie examples of geniuses, such as the stilted and arrogant Sheldon Cooper on *Big Bang Theory*, or the socially outcast title character of the film *Good Will Hunting*, but something deeper, infinitely more special, and broadly applicable to our lives.

According to the Collins Dictionary *Language Lovers* blog (2020), ancient Romans believed that every human was born with a special gift, a spirit that was inherently a part of them throughout their entire lifespan. The Romans recognized that this spirit was born with the person, and therefore they created a word that originated from the Latin verb *gignere*, which means to "give birth or bring forth" and forms the root of the modern word *generate*.

The Romans believed we each have a very special element of our core selves which is individual and innate. It makes us *separate* and *uniquely special* from every other human who has existed, currently exists, or will exist, core to us and us alone.

This was each person's genius. This was each person's contribution to the world.

As you know, the Romans came and eventually fell. The word genius continued to evolve along with human society.

Eventually, genius evolved from being used to describe each person's innate core to describing individual talents; a person might be "a genius" in language, music, organization, numbers, etc.

When this word crossed over into the English language, it was used as such. Eventually, however, humans became uncomfortable with the concept of individualization. As society organized itself to be modern and industrialized, individuals (and their individual talents) were devalued in favor of *rationalizing* (code for clumping individuals together for efficiency purposes) operations.

Rationalizing operations was the key to the modern, scientific management of—well, everything. The *innate remarkableness of each individual* was not important, not recognized, and frankly, was believed to get in the way of the march towards efficiency and productivity.

Occasionally, a person might appear who displayed a *certain very visible knack*. They were labeled as geniuses.

Since Roman times, genius shifted from describing *the element which makes each of us separate and uniquely special* from others to describing only certain people who were somehow different from the rest.

I think it's time that every individual takes back their genius.

SEPARATING OURSELVES FROM THE DEFAULT: MEET YOUR GENIUS

As noted, individuality is the key to getting people out of default mode operating systems, the wiring our brains have that makes us believe our survival is dependent on others.

This lends itself to a default togetherness that ends up circulating anxious energy, prompting our AYs to demand we subsume our individuality even more for survival.

This becomes a downward spiral of us losing access to our genius.

After all, your genius, also known as your "I," is your capacity to separate yourself from others (and their anxious energy), based on your clear thinking and your determined direction for yourself (Titleman 2014).

Put differently, your genius can also be described as your capacity to be an individual while functioning as a part of a group, or your ability to act for yourself without being selfish while acting for others without being selfless (Titleman 2014).

Some researchers call this "differentiation of self" or "self-differentiation" (Titleman 2014).

I like genius better.

Your genius gives you the capacity to determine a thoughtful, goal-directed path for your life that is separate from your default, survival-based, AY response. It enables you to be a free agent in operating with others, serving as a shield from others' AY default functioning.

You access your genius by not accepting the initial path of the default mode and considering a different, more thoughtful response. It means being able to determine, and share directly, your "I" position:

- "This is what I think or believe."

And...

- "This is what I will do or not do."

All without pushing your values or beliefs on others. Your "I" position reflects you taking responsibility for your happiness, comfort, and outcomes, avoiding blame and holding others responsible for what is yours, and encouraging the same in others.

Every single person has their own genius. Your genius can only be defined by you and is not defined by others or by anything external.

You may, like me, (because of deep-rooted patterns) be excellent at solving others' problems. You may use much of your energy to serve others and be who they want you to be. This is not your individual genius.

Others' reactions to you and approval of you do not define your individual genius. You can still care for and be connected to them, but also separate because, like the Romans believed (and they were right!), this "I" exists separate from others, separate from any other human and whether they are happy with you.

To access your genius, you must be able to see and define yourself as separate from others, no matter how important they are to you.

I'll stretch the definition even further to add that this innate, individual genius inside each person is like True North on a compass; it serves as the *ne plus ultra* guide to who we are. Too often, this genius gets dulled, tuned out, or otherwise manipulated by others—particularly when we are melded.

You know what else gets in the way of our "I" despite its necessity for managing our body budget? Yep, you got it: *AY*.

AY is all about managing the body budget to keep us alive. Its base and only instinct is survival.

When we can move *beyond* what *appear* to be survival needs, we access our genius.

WHY INDIVIDUAL GENIUS?

We have a lot of work to do. We need all hands on deck.

As our bodies have become more complex, so have our brains and, as a direct result, our societies. With this complexity comes challenges. All inhabitants of Earth in the twenty-first century face complex problems.

These challenges require us to engage our best thinking; the world needs more geniuses. Specifically, each one of us moving beyond our AY's first response and engaging the clear, non-melded, non-anxious, energy-fueled thinking.

AY might appear to be keeping us alive; after all, ensuring our survival in the short term is its prime directive. Yet, paradoxically, our AYs—while driving us in the direction of *togetherness* in the short term—also stand in the way of clear thinking and effective collaboration in the long term.

Basically, we are getting on each other's nerves and it isn't helping us work together effectively to deal with our Thanos or Elephant threats, and this encourages Narcissus threats.

In the world we live in today, we cannot afford to be distracted by melding and the way the resulting anxious energy provokes our Survival Six. We lose valuable time and opportunity—not to mention brain space for innovation and ingenuity—because anxious energy interrupts our ability to have high-functioning relationships.

The only way to respond effectively to the challenges we face is to create space for everyone's individuality: their individual genius or "I." We don't have a dearth of creative, courageous leaders, or highly capable, multi-faceted followers. As a result of our anxious energy, we just can't see they exist right in front of us.

As we've already seen, anxious energy and *melding* from anxiety-induced *togetherness* disrupt clear thinking. Subsuming people's individuality (their genius) at work *appears* to decrease anxious energy at first (think of the herding instinct of animals banding together against a threat). However, this ends up—in the long term—creating an impermeable "we"

that provokes each person's AY and eventually stanches creativity and innovation (Carmella et al., 1996).

Creativity and innovation are *least* likely to thrive in environments where *togetherness* is the default, which eventually
provokes everyone's AY. Organizations that obsess over hiring
for "cultural fit" or who insist that their workplace *is a family*
create an illusion of *togetherness* that at first appeals to our
AY's desire for simplicity and survival. However, this ends up
provoking our AY when we feel stifled as individuals, feeding
anxious energy into the relationship network.

Constantly high levels of anxious energy negatively impact
our thinking and contribute to allostatic load. Chronic stress
doesn't just impact our creativity—it dulls our thinking and
harms our own physical health (McEwen, 2002).

We have control over this process.

Recall that if one person inside an organization can step
back from the anxious energy circulating throughout the
relationship network, start seeing the anxious energy flow,
and step outside of their patterns within, this serves as a
powerful interruption of the anxious energy.

That is the power of individual genius.

That person, drawing from their genius, begins to act in more
autonomous ways, *participating less*—in an unexamined
default manner—in the anxious energy of the system, and
therefore *inviting others* to do the same.

We may all have our AYs, whose job is to manage the body budget and keep us alive, but we are different from animals in one key respect: we can observe what is going on around us, and using the wonderful abstraction abilities in our brains, we can choose a different response from our default mode (Bowen 1978). We can choose genius mode.

This sets the stage to transform the relationship network, one less anxious-energy and default mode-fueled person at a time. It creates space for us to see others' geniuses, and for them to think beyond their AYs to be more genius themselves. Ultimately, people can do their best thinking, best work, and produce the best results.

Our individual genius is an impermeable barrier to relationship fusion, anxious energy, and the Survival Six. What's more, it enables us to be more...us. Because we can each be more "I."

RE-ACQUAINTING WITH OUR GENIUS

Our genius encompasses the values and beliefs that guide us and enable us to trust ourselves, our self-defined purpose (what McKeown (2014) describes as our "Essential Purpose") and our principles.

Let's unpack this unnecessarily intimidating word: Principles are what *I* as an *individual* think is the "right way to be" in any given situation. They are the fundamental truths that underlie our belief systems. They guide our behavior, what we will or will not do.

We shouldn't be intimidated by this word, even though, to be honest, it seems like a word that appears on a cheesy motivational poster in some random conference room. I invite you to not think of this word in such an abstract way.

Rather, principles are active elements of our lives. Think of them as the self-determined basis for how you will or will not operate —and this is the important part—*before you are faced with the challenge.*

When we define our way of operating *before* facing a challenge, we are far less likely to get caught up in the anxious energy in the moment. We have access to our genius. We are far less likely to allow others to blow us off course (we can maintain our boundaries), and we are even far less likely to blow others off course (not overstep our boundaries with others).

We are less likely to be negatively impacted by a person or an environment that is toxic (where there are no boundaries) or to push toxicity on others.

GENIUS IN ACTION

A client of mine, Julian, has recently been named president of his organization. He'll be solely responsible for the operations of his organization, yet must still answer to his current supervisor, Victoria, and a Board of Directors.

Victoria has strong overfunctioning tendencies and very strong opinions on what it takes for a person to be a successful President. She's served in the role herself and is intelligent, driven, and committed. She has been a tour de force for the organization.

She has made it very clear that she believes Julian should act like her to be successful in his role. In fact, Victoria has a very prescriptive view of how a President should be, even down to wardrobe.

Julian is wildly talented and has earned successively more challenging roles through his gravitas, intelligence, and superb relationship skills. He's the full package and has what it takes to excel in his new position.

There's just one problem. Victoria has blinders on as a function of her AY. She has a hard time not melding with Julian and seeing where she ends and he begins. She believes Julian represents her "self" despite being his own person. As a result, she puts tremendous pressure on Julian to operate according to her values and principles.

Her measure of Julian being successful is not objective, but rather, based on how much he does things like her.

As a result, Julian feels a significant amount of relationship pressure from Victoria to embody this new role precisely as she did. Victoria is constantly in his ear (and, not for nothing, everyone else's), pressuring him to think, talk, act, make decisions, run meetings, and treat others just like she did or would if she were in that position.

When her voice isn't literally in his ear, she has permanently lodged herself in his mind. He has a hard time escaping her anxious energy and the pressure it creates on him.

Julian is an exceptional professional who has the capacity to bring his innate individual genius to his role, if he can only resist the extreme pressure to be just like Victoria. This seems so simple, but it's hard to do because the relationship pressure is so intense.

Taking a step back, it seems a little bit ridiculous. What is the point of Julian being President only to be just like Victoria? What is the individual value—the individual genius—that Julian brings to the role if he is just going to be like her?

Luckily, Julian realizes this. He can see the anxious energy flowing around his relationship network. He doesn't blame Victoria for her over-involvement and the pressure she exerts on him and others. He sees her behavior without judgment, as her patterned anxious energy response.

What does he do?

He does his best to be an individual while remaining in the relationship network with Victoria and the many others operating according to their AYs around him.

He determines a thoughtful, goal-directed path for himself that is created as much as possible outside of his AY's default mode. He takes the time to define for himself what he thinks and believes makes a President successful, and what he will or will not do regardless of the pressure that Victoria and others put on him.

He does this accepting that others have different views than him. He accepts their views as being theirs and continues to move forward on his goal-directed path as an individual and for the organization.

Furthermore, he does his best to not blame, or make others responsible for what happens to him. He tries not to automatically engage in Survival Six behaviors, knowing that they just circulate more anxious energy around the relationship network.

Julian approaches his new role, and all the pressure and anxious energy in the network, like a Navy SEAL. Specifically, he defines his mission. He goes in, accomplishes his mission, and then he moves on, preferably to a different relationship network that has a little less anxious energy flowing around it.

He observes Victoria, including her anxious energy-fueled default behaviors, and tries not to label her, but to see her functioning as a result of the network that they are both in.

He is realistic but hopeful about what is possible, given how strongly Victoria defines his success per her own preferences. He also prepares himself for disappointing her; he knows that Victoria won't always like how Julian defines success and how he embodies his genius in his role as President. He does his best—and this is the hard part—to not let her displeasure throw him off course from achieving his mission.

Think about Navy SEALs. No matter what their mission is, their goal is to get in, accomplish the task, and get out as quickly and safely as possible. They plan, rehearse, think through contingencies, and then execute. This is necessary to operate in a challenging environment.

You may not be in a war zone, but relationship pressure is incredibly intense. Victoria is not going to change. Julian is the one who has the responsibility to maintain his genius despite her strong preferences. If she is in the organization, he will feel tremendous relationship pressure from her to be like him. Instead of trying to change her, he will focus on what he has control over: himself through his "*I*." His biggest asset: his genius.

Furthermore, the more Julian taps into his genius, the more he can impact others (i.e., be a leader, in the most meaningful sense) and short-circuit the anxious energy rocketing around his relationship network. This creates the space for more genius to emerge in the people around him.

THE POWER OF GENIUS

At the heart of genius is integrity, doing our best to remain impermeable and whole—even in the face of relentless pressure from others.

Integrity is the ability to operate maturely and effectively in relationships with others and less under the automatic guesses (and delusions) of our AY. Integrity is being clear about our beliefs, values, and principles (our "I"). It's also our ability to be responsive to our environments without having the anxiety and reactivity of others trigger our own AY.

In genius mode, we don't automatically get pulled into the vortex of **our** AYs. Further, our genius prevents us from being automatically pulled into the vortex of **other peoples**' AYs.

Instead, we define and carry out our genius' mission. We become clear about *who* is responsible for *what* (Lerner 2014).

We move out of default mode and into genius mode.

Then something interesting happens: we also become *leaders*.

In the words of Warren Bennis, to have true credibility with others, we must be "makers of our own lives," which just might be the most difficult task of our lives (Kouzes & Posner 2011, p. 43).

It's ironic, right? The best relationships—and the highest credibility and esteem—come from being who we are, separate from, but still connected to others, on our self-defined paths.

That's the power of genius.

A REAL BOY

—

Geppetto sleeps soundly on the bed, accompanied by his cat Figaro. On the other side of the room, Jiminy Cricket cannot believe his eyes, for a Fairy has appeared. Bathed in all-appropriate magic and starlight, she greets the sleeping Geppetto warmly, assuring him in his slumber that his good works have earned him his wish: Pinocchio can be a real boy.

Crossing the room, she gently steps towards the diminutive puppet, and with a wave of her wand declares softly, nearly in a lullaby:

"Little puppet made of pine,

Wake...

The gift of life is now thine."

Pinocchio stirs awkwardly, with surprise. He tests out his new limbs and cheers loudly.

He wonders how he is alive. The Fairy assures him that she has given him life, with a caveat. He must first pass her tests to become a real boy: "To make Geppetto's wish come true is entirely up to you. Prove yourself brave, true, and unselfish and someday you will be a real boy!"

***

I love the concept of "today years old." It's a new way of describing the moment a person first realizes something important. For example, a person is "today years old" when they learned the new thing they just learned.

This is such a fun phrase, and it also represents an interesting concept: we can be totally reborn (or, actually, have our brains re-wired) as a result of knowledge gained.

I'll never forget the day I was "today years old" in realizing something very important: my husband (and everyone else) is not an extension of me. He is his own person. Unlike Pinocchio, he did not have to prove himself brave, true, and unselfish to earn this right. He is *allowed*, merely because he *is* real.

Sounds obvious, doesn't it? But this is where the storyline of Pinocchio and real life converges.

Many of us think of others all around us as extensions of ourselves, who earn their autonomy (their "self" - the non-puppet form of realness) based on the conditions of their performance. Our children represent us when they are excelling. If our team at work does something amazing, we bask in their glory (never mind when things don't work out).

This starts when we are young. Many of us grew up in households where we represented our families in public. We weren't just who we are, but representatives of our larger clans at school, at church, and everywhere else. When you grow up in an area where everyone knows everyone, this phenomenon is quite common.

As teenagers, we might be embarrassed by our parents. We haven't completed the process of separating from them, of seeing ourselves as different and differentiated.

As adults, we tend to retain this way of defining ourselves in relation to those around us. When those around us are doing well, we gain "self" - like a blood transfusion when we gain fresh, oxygenated blood - and we feel rejuvenated

When those around us struggle, it makes us anxious. We are mortified that they represent us and our brand. We fear they will drag us down with them. This is like a blood loss.

Think for a second how often we think of other people as extensions of ourselves. We define ourselves in relation to them. We assess how *we are doing* based on how *they are doing.*

This is a melded way of thinking. It's also nerve-wracking. Try as we might, we cannot control others.

Whether others are your team at work, your family (including your children), or your spouse/partner or friend, they are not extensions of you. They are their own independent entities.

In a world full of automatic togetherness and melding this line is often blurred.

TRUE EQUALS

My husband jokes with me that he is "the reacher" in our relationship, and I "settled" for him (a joke from a TV show). At first this was flattering and cute. But over time, I realized that him putting himself in this *position* in our relationship was not helpful for either of us. It also was likely provoked by my presence in some way.

As a person full of anxious energy, my own tendency to see those around me as supporting players in my off-off-off Broadway show, entitled *Prove Yourself to Others*, probably didn't help. Not for nothing, this show was having an award-winning, multi-decade, daily performance inside my head.

When we combined the constant loop of this show inside my head with my husband's adorable "aw shucks" Midwestern modesty, you can practically predict the future: I was going to see him not as his own person, but as an extension of me. As a result, he was regularly co-opted into playing a (supporting, of course) role in all my relationships: family, work, friends. And that supporting role was "Most Likely to Make Me Look Good."

Here's the thing: he was (and still is) damn good at it!

Variations of this role have popped up in the most unexpected places: when he would reliably show up at any number of events as my "sidekick," including book readings for books he'd never read, dinners with friends he had little in common with, events with family members who hadn't been very friendly to him, and other activities that didn't align with his personality or interests.

I took it for granted that this was what he was *supposed* to do. He seemed comfortable putting himself in that position, and I didn't give it a second thought otherwise.

His generosity of time and self has been lovely (thanks for the blood, honey!), and (later) horrifying. Specifically, it was horrifying when I was "today years old" and realized that I never really asked him one time if he wanted to do any of these things. I just assumed that he did, and that was that.

After talking to him about this, the overwhelmingly good news is that he enjoyed being with me at these events, for the most part. The only exception was when he felt I had specific standards for his performance: when I wanted him to be something more than "arm candy" and wanted him to project a certain specific air.

That made sense to me, because I recall those events—higher-stakes outings with work colleagues and difficult family members—as not being as enjoyable as they could be.

Why? Because I wasn't viewing him as the amazing, intelligent, quirkily witty, handsome person that he is *on his own*, but as an extension of me. My anxious energy, and its resultant desire to control and rigidity made it hard for us to have fun at these events.

I was depriving both of us of an enjoyable time, all in my AY's attempt to manage what appeared to Yoda as situations with serious implications for my long-term survival when they were not.

STAGE MANAGERS AND SIDEKICKS

In case you think that this only happens in personal relationships, I'm here to paint a picture of many anxious energy-filled executives I've known and worked with.

Enter the Stage Manager.

The Stage Manager types I've known are highly accomplished, visible leaders who have accelerated through the ranks based on their intelligence, decisiveness, and ability to get results. They often have a capacity for interpersonal warmth and a natural charisma that belies their true ambition.

Stage Managers know that their quest for world domination necessitates intelligent, capable, results-oriented, and interpersonally effective people around them. They search far and wide to find the *very best* individuals to serve on their teams.

They also generally keep a few other useful individuals around them who primarily serve another key function: making them feel good.

Sometimes the Stage Manager gets lucky and finds the holy grail: incredibly talented yet insecure individuals who serve both purposes.

The Stage Manager will do anything to hold on to these people, as they are incredibly valuable to them. They may even jeopardize their own career, reputation, and team results to essentially hold these people (and their careers) hostage by convincing them to stick around, beyond which they still contribute to the team.

Occasionally, the Stage Manager outgrows these individuals, and they no longer have value to them as they once did. This can turn into an incredibly painful situation for both the Stage Manager and those they have surrounded themselves with. The individuals left behind may feel as though they did something wrong to have fallen out of good graces with the Stage Manager (and of course, being human, they may have made a mistake along the way that could provide the reason).

But the truth is, they are left behind because they no longer serve their original purpose: providing the Stage Manager with the feeling of being admired, all the while trading their individuality to contribute to the Stage Manager's sense of self.

They were giving blood on the daily. The Stage Manager was sucking it up like a vampire.

Now, the person serving the Stage Manager is very capable of being more autonomous, and often actively chooses not to execute this autonomy for their own AY-fueled reasons. They might be afraid of *being seen* beyond a right-hand person role for the Stage Manager.

Maybe they have their own self-doubts and prefer to stay in a (supposedly) less-demanding situation. These reasons often predictably dovetail with other financial and practical reasons to stick to the one down position in the relationship.

It's possible they haven't yet realized they play this sidekick role so well that it has subsumed their individuality and stolen their blood. At some point, however, they typically start having doubts.

I've met many sidekicks. Their Stage Manager supervisors regularly turn their high-level attention from key issues to impose upon them last-minute changes to a PowerPoint, dictate (in real-time) what their team members should say in an important meeting, and take credit for the great ideas of those who work for them.

In one memorable story, a Stage Manager CEO asked his direct report to accept an external award on his behalf. After working on many drafts of remarks with the internal marketing team, the direct report gave this "officially-sanctioned" speech. However, when internal company communications reported on the award, all mention of the recipient's speech and public appearance was erased, replaced instead by a photo of the CEO and his own comments about the award (written in a way to suggest that it was the CEO that participated in the public acceptance).

According to newsletter, it was as if the public acceptance never occurred, and the executive who accepted the award was completely inconsequential, which is precisely how he felt working for the Stage Manager!

When those who work for Stage Managers finally decide to unplug the IV and look for other opportunities, they often meet with incredible resistance and claims of disloyalty from the Stage Manager. It turns out the Stage Managers have a hard time letting go of their stars.

A PEEK BEHIND THE CURTAIN

The Stage Manager is borrowing individuality or self to manage their anxious energy (Gilbert 2006). They obtain this from both the stars and "hangers on" who are their supporting characters. The Stage Manager may not respect boundaries, and cannot see clearly where they end and others begin.

Others, particularly their direct reports, do not just represent them, but are near literal *extensions* of them (i.e., sources of blood).

This makes it incredibly challenging for everyone around them—particularly those reporting to the Stage Manager—to act as individuals. In fact, those who are naturally more autonomous may chafe at the idea of working for a Stage Manager type. By contrast, those who find the Stage Manager supervisor as appealing find that their over-sized personalities donate self to them, creating a symbiotic relationship.

It proves quite difficult for others to bring their unfiltered ideas, creativity, and diverse perspectives to the Stage Manager, as this is expressly the opposite of what is desired: to serve the Stage Manager's needs first and foremost (and potentially this could be their only function).

More senior leaders in the Stage Manager's orbit often struggle to develop, share, and act upon their own leadership visions, because they are so overwhelmingly preoccupied with serving in their prime directive role: to support the Stage Manager and, above all else, make the Stage Manager feel and look good. As a result, they may appear to others as less-than-fully-functional leaders.

They may find themselves exceptionally stressed or burned out by their work, as they have little to no outlets for the individual strengths and perspectives they bring to their role. They may take on additional responsibility to curry favor with the Stage Manager, but may also find that chasing their supervisor's happiness is elusive.

These supporting characters may even begin to lose sight of their strengths and what is important to them. They may settle for emulating the Stage Manager as much as possible, to avoid standing out in a negative fashion and drawing their ire.

Think about the amazing Stephen King book and film *Misery* (1987). The unstable fan Annie Wilkes purposefully holds the novelist Paul Sheldon hostage to serve her own purposes. At first, she is "helpful," but she soon becomes dangerously controlling, imprisoning Paul and forcing him to do her bidding. In attempting to escape, Paul descends into desperate measures, fighting back against Annie to save himself and regain his freedom and autonomy.

While the more dramatic plot elements of *Misery* are thankfully rare in the business environment, there are still lessons to be gleaned from the film. Specifically, those with Stage Manager tendencies may want to examine the way they engage in thinking of the talented and useful individuals around them as their objects to serve their purposes primarily or solely.

The desire to control others may stem from the Stage Managers' own anxious energy. Their AYs believe that maximum control is necessary, as *they* (and they only) are single-handedly responsible for ensuring that everything goes smoothly, and that requires control over everything and everyone.

Their Yodas believe that perfection in everything (and everyone) is necessary for survival.

The Stage Manager may have a hard time not melding with others. As a result, the supporting characters end up contributing their individuality to soothe the Stage Manager's AY.

The process may replicate itself several times within the hierarchy of an organization, particularly if a Stage Manager is CEO or in the C-Suite.

In this situation, the C-Suite Stage Managers will overstep boundaries with their direct reports, who may then do the same, all to give blood back to their own supervisor. The process then can easily replicate itself downstream throughout the organization.

Stage Managers may instinctively seek direct reports that agree to this exchange of blood, and who may be willing to give up their individuality in exchange for soothing the anxious energy of their supervisor.

Such individuals may not feel they are giving up anything; they may feel especially drawn to being valuable to the Stage Manager, and may crave the Stage Manager's validation to build up their own fragile sense of self.

Often, supporting characters tire of the constant blood donations. Frustrated with the situation, they may engage in Survival Six behaviors that are manifestations of this frustration, but appear as character flaws to those who don't see their actions as a *symptom* of anxious energy.

OVERCOMING THE ILLUSION: FOR THOSE OBSESSED WITH CALLING THE SHOTS

What if you find yourself in the position of being a Stage Manager at work? First, appreciate the fact that you can see that you may have an issue here. Recognition is truly the first step towards trying a new approach.

Second, as best as you can, attempt to separate the *what* from the *how.*

Specifically, it's vital that you codify and hold people accountable through clear standards and expectations on *what* the person does (their technical work/skills).

But do you also have very rigid (and unnecessary) expectations on *how* the person does these things? A quick guide would be to ask yourself: *do I require this person to do things my way, or be just like me and appear according to my standards?*

Standards and expectations are reasonable (and quite frankly, necessary) for *what* someone produces at work. You are paying people to accomplish tasks; this is a matter-of-fact exchange. But if you have very specific expectations for the way they do these things or how they show up at work, you might be a Stage Manager.

What that means for you is you are missing out on some vital genius in the person you are stage managing *that could end up benefiting you tremendously in the long run.*

In any event, even if allowing them to do things their own way doesn't directly help you, it has a vital impact on *them* that has incredible indirect benefits. Specifically, you aren't inviting burnout and cut-off (not to mention great resentment) because you have sucked the blood out of others unnecessarily.

Third, try some reflection:
- *How realistic is it for me to see others as mere extensions of who I am versus individuals who have responsibility for themselves, and who have a right to be who they are?*
- *Do I demand or somehow place expectations on others to show up precisely how I want them to show up, without this really being necessary?*
- *How does this build me up?*
- *Do I get unreasonably upset if they don't do this?*
- *How could it be damaging to them in the long term?*
- *How much may I be preventing people from being individuals?*
- *And, perhaps most importantly: am I confident enough in who I am that if someone who works for me makes a mistake, I can take responsibility for my part without fearing that I'll be rejected by people I'm trying to impress?*

OVERCOMING THE ILLUSION: IS THAT YOU, SUPPORTING CHARACTER?

Ironically, the advice to a person working with/for a Stage Manager is quite similar to the advice for the Stage Manager themselves, since both being a Stage Manager and feeding into the Stage Manager dynamic stems from the same place: a desire to decrease your anxious energy, along with decreasing the anxious energy of others (at least temporarily).

Your AY is driving this process. How does it serve their (likely misinterpreted) need for survival at all costs?

Specifically, you may feel that you must give blood (give up self) to gain the approval from others. Approval that you could just give yourself.

Some suggestions:
- Take some time to rediscover, reconnect, and/or rebuild your individuality. Seek opportunities to differentiate yourself from those around you, particularly those you perceive as senior to you or as authority figures.
- Resist the temptation to go along with a Stage Manager just to lessen tension between you and them. Consider your *own* thoughts/opinions about the situation, and then share them without apologizing for being who you are.
- If you find yourself engaging in anxious-energy fueled behaviors that are hallmarks of high-stress environments, such as gossip, cliques, blaming, or singling others out, ask yourself: Do I really think these things or want to go along with others in engaging in these behaviors, or am I doing these things to lessen the anxiety of those around us?
- Use your awareness of these activities occurring around you as evidence that anxiety/reactivity is high, and there's a good chance that stage managing is occurring.

OTHERS ARE ALLOWED TO BE REAL

As a recovering Stage Manager, I've been fortunate enough to gain enough insight through reflecting upon my relationship with my husband.

The more I stepped back, the more his individual genius stepped forward, and it delivered with ideas to solve problems, witty jokes, and a different, unique perspective. The more I enjoyed these surprises, (which existed all along, though I couldn't see them), the more I'd ask myself: Does he have enough opportunity to be this amazing person in our relationship? Do I give him this space?

We could ask the same things of ourselves regarding those around us in organizations:

I completely understand why our AYs want the people we spend the most time around, whether they are our loved ones or colleagues, to be as much like us as possible. This *makes things easier* for our AY, though it isn't necessary. This is merely our *preference*, which our brains have turned into a must have.

Your AY will also take as much from another person as it can get. It makes things easier for them.

Geniuses separate their "selves" from others.

When I separated my "self" from my husband, we became closer, and our relationship became more fun and interesting. It was lighter and more equal, which led to better outcomes.

Freed up from supporting me all the damn time, his career experienced a huge "glow-up." Suddenly he had time and energy to invest all that genius into his further professional development, and this time and effort was being rewarded by others, which benefited both of us.

As you can imagine, my AY likes this very much.

My husband isn't a puppet made from pine. I had to stop pulling his strings. I didn't need a fairy with a magic wand to make him real. Unlike Pinocchio, he didn't need to earn his autonomy. He was entitled to it as a human adult separate from me—separate, but connected.

This way is better for everyone. Free the Pinocchios in your life and see how they might surprise you.

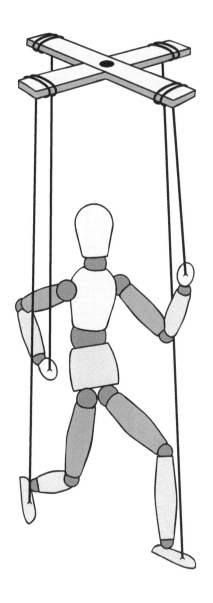

SCOOBY SNACKS

———

Ninety-nine billion dollars: that is what Americans spent on their pets last year, more than double what they spent a decade ago (Mitic 2021).

This number isn't that surprising given how valuable our pets are to us. They are our loyal companions and cuddle buddies. We feel love from them, and we enjoy giving our love to them and taking care of their needs. Compared to human relations, our relationship with our pets is simple and uncomplicated.

Harry Truman is often mistakenly quoted saying: "If you want a friend in Washington, get a dog." (Pflaum 2016). Even though Truman disliked pets, the original point is still valid: in a world full of complicated relationships, having a pet is simple and rewarding.

As wonderful as pets are—full stop—they are also an incredible window into understanding the powerful motivator of *approval and reward*, particularly how often we rearrange our relationships, and even our whole existence, to gain approval (i.e., our own treats) from others.

This is an invitation for us to consider how often we ask other people to be approval vending machines (Smith 2019), and how we'll contort ourselves into pretzels seeking rewards from others even if it doesn't end up being what is best for us.

A client recently welcomed two adorable Yorkies into her family, a brother and sister duo. They are sweet, loyal, and charming, but one has anxious and reactive tendencies towards strangers. The client hired one of the best dog trainers in NYC to deal with this reactivity.

Her advice? Give the dog treats to reward non-reactive behavior and keep giving them until the desired behavior is reinforced.

My client took the advice and started plying the pups with treats when they complied with her commands. Voila! Her anxious pup became a little angel.

Her pup isn't the only one that loves to receive rewards for behavior deemed desirable to others; we humans do this too. Recall that our brains are wired for *togetherness* for survival purposes, and we crave acceptance, approval, and validation from others.

We love our "Scooby Snacks" of belonging and validation (Frei & Morriss 2020a).

At what cost do we earn these treats, however?

A powerful, innovative, and thoughtful C-Suite leader I interviewed for this book mused to me that he became far more successful, far more creative, and far more comfortable with himself when he stopped mindlessly joining groups and seeking their approval. He likened joining these groups to joining a country club.

Like a country club, every group has some type of cost associated with joining it. Unlike a country club, the costs of joining these other types of groups may not be as obvious upfront, but may be far more insidious.

The costs such as having to give up, hide, or jettison some part of our individuality may be incurred personally, and that's just for being accepted into the group. Acceptance alone still may not be enough to earn respect from those already in the group!

We all might take a step back occasionally to consider what costs we are *truly paying* to be a part of any relationship or group and whether those costs are too high, or just not worth it.

We face plenty of opportunities to lose ourselves in melding or togetherness every day. We may have gained some self—a temporary blood transfusion—as a result, but how much blood have we also given just to belong or to somehow make others happy?

We've discussed individuality—our genius. You know what our genius isn't?

Genius is not what Smith (2019) calls the Four A's: Attention, Assurance, Approval, and Agreement. Those come from others; they don't reflect who we are at our core. Some scholars call this "pseudo-self," and describe it as the part of a person that is negotiable. It can change depending on who we are around (Smith 2019).

I like to call this "faux self."

"Faux self" is the approval/reassurance from those closest to us (including our partners), praise and approval from others, titles, and even gaining self through constant busyness.

Faux self is like the façade of a building in an old western movie. It exists, but it isn't solid.

It can help us deal with our anxious energy and the anxious energy of those around us, but when this process is in motion, we are borrowing (or lending) calmness. It doesn't work to truly help us feel better about ourselves.

As Smith (2019) notes, "when we give people the power to raise our functioning, we also give them the power to deflate us like a bouncy castle" (p. 25).

Sometimes, instead of seeking the approval of society, we may seemingly exist to please one person in life, often a partner, parent, or highly influential friend. Tim Urban (2014) calls this person a Puppet Master because their approval is so important that they generally end up running our lives.

We seek their approval nonstop, living in fear of upsetting them and doing anything to avoid it. The Puppet Master casts a long shadow on all our decisions, determines our opinions, and even encroaches on our beliefs.

Let's look at how the Four A's played out for Luka.

LUKA'S DILEMMA

Luka is a senior partner in a Big Four professional services firm. In many ways, he is a rockstar: intelligent, thoughtful, and dedicated. He's a bit brusque for some people, but can back it up with "the goods."

He achieved fabulous success early in his career, a true "egghead of eggheads." Luka moved up the ranks rapidly, establishing himself as a luminary in his area of specialty. Think: the lawyer that lawyers go to when they have a question.

He drafted rules and policy that eventually guided his peers' technical work and became enshrined as an industry standard. He is literally writing the book (well, at least, some of the policies/standards in the book) for his profession. In addition to serving his own clients, he also consults on complex matters that involve his specialized expertise around the world.

Luka does well when he has the opportunity to be a part of the professional practice experts within his organization. His specialized talents thrive here and others appreciate him.

That office, however, is in Manhattan. Luka's wife doesn't want to live in NYC; her preference is that they raise their children out west, which fits significantly better for their lifestyle preferences. Their family relocates accordingly. Now he lives on the West Coast, and virtual work isn't an option.

When Luka leaves the specialized group, he loses some of his shine. He isn't as naturally inclined to excel as a "line partner." He doesn't believe it challenges him enough. He does well financially, but he's on edge and unhappy. He escapes into his work, seeking attention for his specialized skills.

He says yes to last-minute opportunities to contribute his specialized expertise in some exotic locale, much to the ire of his local boss. He feels he needs to do these things to keep his sanity.

Day-to-day technical work is less satisfying for Luka. His approach, which was so valuable when consulting on a complex matter, is a little too intense for more typical clients. At times, he inadvertently insults or angers them, and his boss, Jake, has to step in and smooth things over.

Jake detests having to run interference for Luka and resents the time Luka spends on work outside the local office. He feels Luka isn't doing enough in support of developing local business, which is his top priority.

Their AYs regularly clash.

Despite this, Luka feels he is, as they say in the poker world, "pot-committed." He feels circumstances have compelled him to keep his current hand. He doesn't think he can afford to make a change in lifestyle and is very committed to staying put. The West Coast is the only place his wife and kids want to be, and he cares deeply about making them happy.

However, Luka is grumpy. Unsurprisingly, this spills over to his wife and kids. It affects their mood and behavior too.

Luka feels temporarily better when he gets the attention, assurance, and approval of his colleagues as Mr. Fix-It, but he feels empty when he must do typical work like Jake.

Luka is a polarizing figure inside the office, given his uneven track record with local clients and the time spent on projects elsewhere. By chasing the Four A's, in both his work and family life, Luka feels like he has it all together, but he is slowly chipping away at his credibility. His uneven performance with local clients has lowered his overall reputation in the firm, despite his superb work in other practices.

He has chosen the temporary happiness of others over his genius. He has chosen not to inconvenience others or separate himself from them and their anxious energy-fueled relationship pressure. Ironically, this isn't enough to please them.

Luka's not alone; I've definitely incurred the costs of membership to gain the "Scooby Snacks" of the Four A's.

A PEEK BEHIND THE CURTAIN

Your genius—your "I"—is your capacity to separate yourself from others and their anxious energy based on your clear thinking and determined direction for yourself.

Pleasing others—however noble it appears— is dictated by togetherness and relationship pressure. It stems from direction **from** others, not direction **we determine for ourselves**. Our individual genius does not stem from others approval, or from selfless actions. Recall that our individual genius is inherent in each of us, not determined by the approval, happiness, and validation of others.

Requiring validation and approval from others is the path of the default mode, guaranteed to temporarily soothe AY's survival fears when anyone around us seems upset or full of anxious energy.

This is not the path of genius, however.

Geniuses can deal with the anxious energy of the world, and with the expectations and potential emotional upset of the people around them, with less need to build faux self.

Luka and I pursue the Four A's to relieve ourselves of our anxious energy. We might think that it is far better, in the short term, to pursue approval/acceptance/agreement to keep ourselves and the rest of the people around us happy and calm.

Urban (2014) includes a hilarious cartoon on his blog that perfectly demonstrates this phenomenon: it shows a stick figure accomplishing a massive achievement, and then immediately passing that achievement on to their Puppet Master.

Once you see this process demonstrated by a stick figure cartoon, you can't unsee it all around you in real life, in your own actions, and in the actions of others.

What really goes on when this happens, however, as Dr. Larry Smith (2011) puts it, is that you are effectively conceptualizing that person—your Puppet Master—as your jailer.

If this isn't an extreme version of melding, I don't know what is.

OVERCOMING THE ILLUSION

As we know from earlier chapters, our brains are more complex than dog brains because our bodies are more complex.

While AY's survival needs are temporarily met by the Four A's, our brains are capable of so much more.

Remember, each one of us is a genius.

You access your genius by moving beyond default mode ways of operating, and considering a different, more thoughtful response to anxious energy all around us.

Making choices that aren't right for us just to win the approval, acceptance, or happiness of those around us does not embody our genius.

AY is going to freak out because someone may not approve of or agree with us. This seems like a clear threat to survival, but it's not. Luka's family can thrive in New York City, particularly if Luka is thriving there as an individual.

AY interprets survival threats as needs for others and opens the door to the Four A's. We typically don't realize how much we rely on the faux self that others provide through the Four A's until our supply (derived from others) is interrupted or cut off. In such a situation, we are only left with our anxious energy.

Luka's first step—and ours too, if we find ourselves being deflated by over-reliance on faux self—is to recognize that what we are feeling is being driven by AY's default. However, we can call upon our capacity for more sophisticated thinking.

We don't have to spend our lives chasing our Puppet Master's happiness, even if AY attempts to make us feel this way.

We can define who we are outside of others (while remaining connected to them), separate their emotions from our emotions, and resist the temptation to soothe their anxious energy.

I promise: they can do this themselves if you give them the space!

Being caring and connected but still separate is possible.

We can also recognize when we are a little too willing to soothe our own anxious energy with faux self by recognizing for ourselves what our independently defined real value is to the world.

Every single person has their own genius. Your genius can only be defined by you: not by others, nor by anything external.

Give yourself the Scooby Snack already!

MRS. O'LEARY AND THE MISATTRIBUTION

Imagine being personally blamed for $4.7 billion in damages, or for the deaths of 300 people and the displacement of 100,000 others. What about being labeled the alleged primary cause for the loss of 17,500 buildings and the destruction of 2,112 acres of land in one of the most prominent cities in the country?

This is how it would feel to be Mrs. Catherine O'Leary in 1871. Despite being officially exonerated (along with her cow) 126 years later, Mrs. O'Leary is still blamed for the Great Chicago Fire (Schons 2011).

Fueled by anti-Irish and anti-Catholic sentiment, rumors of O'Leary's pyromania were spread by a newspaper reporter. He claimed that an ill-timed cow kick, a lantern, and the milkmaid's laziness were responsible for the conflagration.

Mrs. O'Leary was poor and a social outcast—the perfect scapegoat! The reporter later recanted, but it was too late; the damage to female and bovine reputations was done.

To this day, no culprit has been uncovered. Several theories abound: a thief attempting to steal milk, gamblers in the O'Leary barn, and meteors.

Reader: when in doubt, blame meteors!

Never mind that Chicago was in an historic drought, and strong winds from the southwest combined with a tinderbox of wood structures produced the perfect set-up for a disaster. And wouldn't you know it, bad luck and human error further contributed to the destruction.

Yet blame still rests squarely on the shoulders and haunches of Mrs. O'Leary and her cow. Our AYs like this simple explanation.

I've encountered my share of Mrs. O'Learys in my time as a consultant and coach. But I'm not going to share their stories.

I'm going to share a happy story about blame.

A C-Suite client of mine, Barb, has a direct report, Kris.

Barb is fabulous. She has exceptional relationships with her team, her peers, and her supervisor, the COO. She's been in her role for almost two years, having been recruited from a competitor to bring her incredible wisdom and energy to revive her division.

Kris, who has been in the organization for a while, is a go-getter with a polarizing style. Kris produces excellent results for her organization and is beloved internally except by Tommy and Sam (who happen to be buddies).

Further complicating the situation, Tommy and Barb's roles overlap, and this produces some friction between the two of them which they thankfully handle well.

Sam (who reports to Barb) has a decent relationship with his boss. He applied for her job but didn't get it and appears to have some lingering resentment.

After a recent re-organization and the departure of two prominent people within the wider relationship network, Tommy and Sam began peppering Barb with complaints about Kris.

Barb asked me for some help on how she could handle the delicate conversation with Kris. I was having a hard time helping Barb, however, because it wasn't clear to me what the issue was with Kris.

So, I asked Barb what substantive, job-related performance issues that Kris was having.

Barb's response: "Great question. I cannot think of any."

I was a little shocked at this point and concerned that I didn't hear Barb correctly. I asked more questions to clarify. Barb confirmed that there were no substantive issues that she could share with Kris.

Nonplussed, I asked her what fueled the complaints about Kris.

"Tommy and Sam haven't been happy with Kris for some time. They just don't like her. But you know, now I realize from talking to you that there is nothing substantial here. There is nothing I can tell her that she needs to change, because she is doing everything she needs to do," Barb responded.

She then cocked her head a bit, and it dawned on her what was occurring within the relationship network. Kris was suffering from a negative reputation with some people in the organization (people who also happen to also have anxious energy-driven relationships with both Kris and Barb).

Barb was prepping to coach Kris on this reputation and was even thinking about having to replace her if the grumbling about her became too loud.

However, once I asked a few questions, Barb realized that there was absolutely nothing substantive that Kris could do to "fix" her reputation with the people who didn't like her.

That was because it wasn't a result of something Kris did (that she could then do differently), it was a function of who Kris is.

Obviously, that can't be fixed.

The good news is that Barb left Kris alone, and Kris continues to be awesome. She continues making many people in the organization very satisfied by achieving the outcomes she is responsible for achieving and doing everything she needs to do to fulfill her role.

Interestingly, since this conversation, Tommy and Sam have been curiously silent about Kris. Maybe it's because things have gotten a little less anxious in the organization?

Barb is happy because she didn't have a difficult conversation. She does have a wider vantage point of some interesting relationship dynamics inside her organization, and now knows to ask specifically what the issue is when people come to her with complaints about her team.

A PEEK BEHIND THE CURTAIN

According to Gilbert (2006), when we blame, we give up responsibility for ourselves and our behavior. We muzzle our ability to see how each of us contributes anxious energy to the relationship network.

Recall that anxious energy circuits around relationship networks, and when threats surface (like the Elephant and Narcissus threats circulating around Barb's network), people start showing postures or symptoms of this anxious energy (the Survival Six).

Blame is one of these postures/symptoms. Our AYs want us to be rid of the survival challenge that anxious energy presents, so we look for a convenient person to blame. Blaming tends to lower the anxious energy temporarily but may become entrenched in the relationship network as a pattern.

Barb noticed that this pattern of blame arose at a curious time: the departures and re-orgs likely provoked increased anxious energy in the network. It needed an outlet, and Kris was it!

People within the relationship network may take on different postures at different times. By themselves these postures are value-neutral, just a way that anxious energy gets blown off by people.

However, the results of these postures can be quite damaging.

Blame is a type of conflict in which one side doesn't see their role in the conflict or doesn't take responsibility for what they contribute (Gilbert 2006).

At times, some people may have what's termed as an *automatic combative-competitive posture*, wherein they become personally insulted by someone who *appears* to be disagreeing with them but is just sharing their thinking. This can breed blame in a network.

Tommy appears to have this posture. His typical response to anyone's point of view is like the iconic line from *Anchorman*: "Well, that escalated quickly."

Another source of blame is *triangling*. For example, Sam may seek to lessen the tension in his relationship with Kris by complaining about her to Barb. He might even complain about Kris to deal with his anxious energy of being around Barb.

Triangles are a common way that people seek to transfer their anxious energy to others. They are unavoidable in human relationships and aren't inherently good or bad. They just happen.

To be true to your genius, it's essential to operate as an individual as much possible within triangles. If you don't operate well within them, this adds anxious energy to the network.

OVERCOMING THE ILLUSION

Let's say one of your team members spends a lot of time blaming another team member. What do you do?

   A: Ignore this; people are just being immature and you don't engage in emotional stuff.
   B: Call a team session so the entire group can discuss performance issues and teamwork; hope that the issue gets resolved when the team has an opportunity to talk through things out in the open.
   C: Have a serious, crucial conversation with the person being blamed; after all, they do have some performance gaps and the responsible thing to do is address them.
   D: Schedule some one-on-one time with the person engaging in blame. Take some time to make contact and find out what is going on with them.

Many leaders try A, B, and C, without much success.

Sometimes they even go all in and get one or more of these individuals an outside coach, presuming that the outside coach will either:

- Help the leader be more direct with either the "blamer" or the "scapegoat."
- Coach the blamer due to how disruptive their gossipy behavior is.
- Coach the scapegoat to help them overcome whatever issues they have.

Remember, coaches and consultants are not omniscient. They may not see the anxious energy flowing around the relationship network.

They also have their own anxious energy; they typically want to produce results and are not immune to relationship postures, particularly overfunctioning. They are humans too!

You may find it counterintuitive, but Gilbert (2006) suggests option D: scheduling one-on-one time with the blamer to gain some insight in what is going on with them.

During this conversation, you are—ideally—not blaming the blamer. Remember, the spread of anxious energy around a relationship network is just what happens with humans. If you can summon a position of curiosity and make nonjudgmental contact with the blamer, you can learn a little more about what is going on.

Gilbert (2006) also suggests including some humor in this conversation, as it can be a highly effective relief valve for anxious energy. However, try to avoid taking an overfunctioning or "know-it-all" posture in this conversation because, remember, no one has all the answers.

That's why you are having this conversation. To find out what's really going on.

A few other pointers:

- See blame as an indicator of anxious energy, like threatening storm clouds rolling across the sky, indicating that a storm is brewing.
- Remember that every human inside an anxious group is approaching it with a relationship posture, including you. Know your postures (the way you deal with anxious energy—check out the Survival Six), recognize

others' postures, and try to think beyond them to determine the right approach for dealing with the real issue.

- Resist the urge to do what you would typically do. What we typically do in times of stress is likely our default posture. What else could you try?
- Understand that people are responsible for their temporary emotional state and feelings. Remember Barrett's (2017) research? Emotions are a function of people's body budget, but our brain makes a (typically not so great) guess that they result from an external cause. The good news is that every human has more control over their emotional response than they probably realize. Try letting others be responsible for their temporary emotional states, knowing that they are indeed, temporary. Avoid getting pushed off course by others' emotional states (or your own).
- Remember that the group leader role models clear thinking for others. Do your best to overcome your AY's default and aim for a curious posture with everyone, even people you disagree with.

Geniuses understand that anxious energy is constantly circulating around and through us, and this often leads to people talking about each other, instead of talking to each other (Gilbert 2006). This doesn't give them much opportunity to directly resolve their issues. Anxious energy impacts communication, which impacts relationships, which in turn degrades communication further in a potentially endless downward spiral.

Geniuses resist this anxious energy to stay connected to the group, even when blame and other Survival Six postures surface.

Like Barb, they avoid premature conclusions, like blaming a milkmaid for an environmental catastrophe.

Operating outside of their AY's default, geniuses can accomplish what the situation requires: being in one-on-one contact with all group members, trying to understand what is going on with the blamer, dealing directly with any performance issues, and modeling open communication.

HELL IS OTHER PEOPLE

———

The year was 1994, and Quentin Tarantino's film masterpiece *Pulp Fiction* had just been released to wide acclaim. It would later be selected for preservation in the National Film Registry for its cultural, historical, and aesthetic significance.

Pulp Fiction is a classic due to Tarantino's innate creativity and unique storytelling. It also masterfully represents the complexity and illusions of life.

Lest you think this film has questionable application to the business world, I posit it is (among other things) an exploration of a "supervisor" and "performer" relationship.

It just so happens that the supervisor is powerful crime boss Marsellus Wallace, and the performer is boxer Butch Coolidge.

Neither Marsellus nor Butch are having the greatest of days. Their AYs are provoked by multiple threats, and they are having a hard time functioning well under the anxious energy flowing around their relationship networks.

Marsellus depended on Butch to throw—or to deliberately lose—his boxing match. Butch didn't, which displeases Marsellus greatly. Marsellus puts a "hit" on Butch for not performing according to his needs.

Butch attempts to flee but has a hard time outrunning Marsellus's performance expectation.

Their life trajectories intersect in a series of unfortunate incidents that ultimately leads to Marsellus having a *very bad experience.*

Wouldn't you know it, Butch's difficult day also ends up being Marsellus's bad day.

My clients have different lifestyles than Butch and Marsellus, but that doesn't mean some of the themes from *Pulp Fiction* do not resonate with their lives.

One client, Jacob, was recently up for partner in a professional services firm.

Like Butch, he is motivated by personal pride and a desire to prove himself. Also, like Butch, he is so caught up in his internal drama he cannot see what else is going on around him, including the problems and drama in the life of his supervisor.

Jacob should have been preparing for the "interview of his life" (a panel interview that would determine whether he would make partner, a.k.a. the most intense job interview scenario you can imagine). But he was full of anxious energy and was resentful of his own boss, Maria.

Two elements of his life, which he had little to no control over, were bothering him. First, he was impatient with the timeline of his promotion, believing he should have been promoted sooner. Second, he was concerned that the anxious energy that radiated from Maria was going to derail his performance at his panel.

Jacob was fixated on pleasing Maria. He was known as a confident, intelligent, technically-savvy professional, but generally collapsed into a puddle of anxious energy around Maria. His lack of confidence would show through in a bit of awkwardness. He would get nervous, talk too much and too loudly, and appear young and inexperienced even though he was a technical whiz.

He just couldn't be himself around her, and he couldn't figure out why. Maria had such an impact on Jacob, she would provoke his AY as if his actual survival was dependent on her approval of him.

He would then get upset at Maria for "doing this to him." He would also get upset with himself for "allowing" himself to be "done in" by her.

Jacob felt that his anxious response to Maria was irrational and problematic, and he worried about how it would impact his reputation with others. He put a lot of pressure on himself to get over it.

Jacob wasn't being irrational, however. Maria had a lot of control over Jacob's livelihood and future. As a result, his AY response to her was completely rational.

But it wasn't just Jacob that had an anxious energy response to Maria—it was everyone. Like Marsellus Wallace, Maria made a lot of people anxious.

She was no gangster, but she was hard to get to know. She had a reputation for being a lone wolf and wasn't particularly receptive to feedback. Maria was a bit cliquey; she had a couple of confidantes she seemed to implicitly trust, but everyone else was cut off. She also displayed a less-than-enthusiastic interest in their ideas, needs, and perspectives.

Overall, Maria was intimidating and closed off. Even her fellow partners expressed frustration with her leadership and direction. While this fact could have provided him with some comfort, Jacob's AY wouldn't let him get out of his own head to see that he wasn't alone.

Jacob believed his unhappiness stemmed from other people. *They* made him anxious. *They* weren't promoting him as fast as he wanted to be promoted. *They* didn't do what they were supposed to do (give his AY relief from the anxiety and uncertainty surrounding his future).

His default mode was to see Maria very one-dimensionally, focusing only on what she was supposedly doing to him. He didn't take a lot of time to think about what was going on in her world, what threats were provoking her own AY, and whether she was having as many bad days as him.

Luckily, Jacob was willing to get more curious about Maria.

Here's what he saw when he finally looked: Maria was dealing with a lot of pressure herself and was filled with anxious energy, just like Jacob. This distorted her thinking and provoked her default mode.

She had very visible Survival Six postures that were symptoms of her high anxious energy, such as trusting only a few people and cutting off from everyone else.

Furthermore, Maria is only human. Therefore, her opinions of Jacob would inevitably have some distortions.

Her opinions and decisions about his career trajectory were not, as we would like them to be, objectively a result of his performance. As much as we hate to admit it, we now know that her view of him was highly influenced by her AY's guesses about people like Jacob.

Until we talked, Jacob couldn't see that Maria had Thanos, Elephant, and—we guessed—Narcissus threats that she was dealing with, and that these threats provoked a lot of anxious energy inside Maria. She was so closed-off. We didn't know this for sure, but when we stood back and looked at some of Maria's functioning, there were plenty of clues that she was full of anxious energy.

Her inability to manage this anxious energy in a functional way meant that it poured into Jacob, as it often ends up in the person who is most insecure in the relationship network. This impacted Jacob's ability to embody his genius around Maria; she was always knocking him off course.

But you know what? It's Jacob's "response ability" to do everything he could to prevent this from happening (Lerner 2014). That is, Jacob has the ability to choose a different response to Maria.

First, he had to let go of the blame and resentment he felt about the promotion timeline.

None of us can go back and fix the past. We can consider the past to the extent that it helps us see patterns of functioning in relationship networks but holding on to past resentments doesn't serve us in the present.

Second, Jacob needed to realize that, while he could control his performance, he couldn't control what others (especially Maria) thought **about** his performance. He could do his best, but it was out of his control whether his best was good enough in Maria's eyes to merit promotion.

There were too many other variables that he didn't have control over. He couldn't control Maria's anxious energy: not about him, or about anything else. Reacting to her anxious energy in his usual way—by becoming more anxious himself—wasn't going to make things better.

He could only control the objective elements of his performance (i.e., the outcomes and results he could achieve), but—and here's where it gets difficult—he couldn't control what his leadership felt about his performance.

Theoretically, Jacob could achieve all his targets—and maybe even blow things out of the water—but this fact in and of itself was not sufficient to change how people felt about his performance, or even about him in general.

All Jacob had control over was his objective work results. He couldn't fix the anxious energy in Maria and the relationship system.

A PEEK BEHIND THE CURTAIN

We love the warm and cozy myth that we live in a meritocracy. The rules seem clear: work hard and get rewarded. Still, hard though it is to accept, Jacob could be amazing at what he does and still not be deemed acceptable enough (or at all) by others.

Jacob is not alone in being subjected to perceived or real unfairness. We've all experienced or will experience this. We are all Jacob.

You might be familiar with the *Stockdale Paradox*. This concept was named for Admiral James Stockdale, a POW imprisoned in the "Hanoi Hilton" during the Vietnam War who endured eight years of humiliation and abuse.

Stockdale miraculously made it through his ordeal, despite not knowing whether he would ever be released or see his family again. He did this by operating according to the following principles: possessing unwavering faith that he could and would prevail in the end, while maintaining the discipline sufficient to confront the most brutal facts of his current reality (Collins n.d.).

By comparison, Jacob's situation was a cakewalk. It still felt incredibly difficult to him, and yet, he had a plan.

Jacob had to do two things:

1. He had to have faith and put in the work to have an awesome panel performance.
2. He also had to be clear-eyed about the facts: his performance could be tremendous yet he could still be held back.

Others under the influence of their AYs might never see Jacob objectively. In this manner, it was possible he wasn't going to get what he deserved.

That is Jacob confronting the "most brutal facts" of his current reality.

Under the influence of AY, Jacob felt that, as Sartre famously put it: "L'enfer, c'est les autres" (Sartre 1958). That is, hell is other people.

At first blush, other people were the source of Jacob's problems.

Jacob was frustrated about the past. Yet he also had to deal with anxious energy in his present, and Maria was always provoking his Survival Six, further damaging his credibility with her.

He was motivated to be promoted in large part because he thought it would give him a more equal footing with her, making him feel less anxious energy around her.

But other partners feel anxious energy around Maria. Everyone does. That's her effect on others.

Her participation in small cliques was a symptom of her anxious energy (Chambers 2009). Maria's inability to act in an open way with individuals who weren't in her inner circle was a flashing red neon sign, displaying her anxious energy for all to see.

Jacob was hoping for a blood transfusion (gaining "self") through his promotion.

Like a hero in a movie, however, Jacob had more than enough self all along. He just needed to unearth his genius by remembering his technical skills and vast experience, revisiting himself in more confident moments, and defining what was truly important to him.

He could remember the core characteristics of himself that made him unique and an incredible member of humanity, regardless of his title.

Hell is not having to work with Maria. We just think that having to work with Maria is Hell because our AYs' fear for their survival around anxious people like Maria.

Unless they draw upon their genius, people around Maria will always show symptoms of anxious energy.

OVERCOMING THE ILLUSION
Maria, although not perfect, isn't the problem.

Jacob has a pattern of increased anxious energy around people like Maria. Until Jacob becomes curious as to why his AY has such a strong response to people like her, he'll continue to think of her as the problem, and not his own reactions to her.

Similarly, in *Pulp Fiction*, Butch may think Marsellus is the problem. However, if you've seen the film, you know Butch was no angel.

Given the dramatic twists and turns in their relationship, Butch and Marsellus are committed to not crossing paths again in the future. However, Jacob and Maria will likely work together for at least another decade or so.

Luckily for Jacob, the longer he worked with Maria, the more interested he was in considering the origins of his anxious energy around her.

He could see his anxious pattern with her play out in other relationships, including with family members. It felt weird when he could see it, but he was unintentionally replaying some of these patterns, trying to work out his own issues with his family through his relationships at work.

Jacob realized that he may never truly be at his best around anxious leaders like Maria unless he jettisoned the debilitatingly impossible task of pleasing her all the time.

In his fixation with her, he lost sight of his genius.

It was far better for him to define and execute the substantive tasks of his role and do this as well as he could, not expecting that everyone (including Maria) would be able to appreciate his genius.

Geniuses take the time to slow down and get curious about how anxious energy flows around their relationship networks, and how this energy impacts them. They see their typical reaction to anxious others. They then try out different responses.

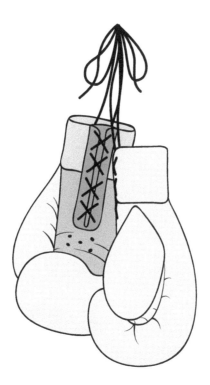

SLENDER SVEN AND MY UNFORCED ERROR

———

At six in the morning, the sunrise was blazing pink and orange as it crept over the Yard. The air was so cold that I could see my breath, and my legs felt numb underneath the thin jogging pants and windbreaker I wore.

I was on my way to triumph over the threats from the Hangry Viking.

Specifically, I was jogging to the Boathouse at the US Naval Academy (USNA). It was the autumn, and I was still getting used to being a Youngster, the Naval Academy term for a sophomore.

Returning to the academy after Plebe year (the horrendous, embarrassing freshman year that lasts approximately ten months but feels like an entire lifetime) is exciting and daunting for every Youngster.

Youngsters have a chance for a fresh start to define themselves beyond being a lowly Plebe.

Further, because we didn't have to spend approximately eighteen hours a day being constantly berated by upper class, we could finally focus more on academics and other activities, including sports.

Plebe year typically begins with Indoctrination (I-Day).

I-Day commences "Plebe Summer": the couple month boot camp for incoming Midshipmen that is designed to prepare them to join the rest of the Brigade at the start of the academic year.

Plebe year ends with the Herndon Climb in May.

Herndon is insane. Picture one thousand or so sweaty, eager, and completely fearless young men and women in standard-issue blue and gold bathing suits and athletic shorts, attempting to climb up a stone obelisk greased with pounds and pounds of pure lard to replace one cover (hat) placed on it with another.

It smells and feels just exactly as bad as you are imagining. Worse, even.

The climb is the *official* end of Plebe year, but Youngsters are typically in a weird identity no-man's land until they return for the next academic year.

From personal experience, it only truly feels like you are no longer a Plebe when you see the new crop of Plebe maniacs running around in the same intentionally bizarre way you did yourself.

This transition, like all transitions, is anxious energy inducing and awkward.

Technically, upper class are second class and Firsties (first class)—juniors and seniors, respectively.

Youngsters are in this weird liminal place: no longer Plebes but not yet upper class.

Combine that with more difficult coursework, higher expectations for military professional development, and the need to prove yourself with your new company; there was a lot of anxious energy circulating around my relationship network.

That's the setting where I found myself on that brisk morning. At USNA, athletic participation is required. Happily, we were encouraged to try a variety of activities.

I sampled accordingly, spending some time on the cycling team and even a few misguided hours on the rugby field (which became out of the question once I figured out I have this weird aversion to people crashing into me at full velocity).

I was drawn to USNA's Crew program because of its excellence: a gorgeous boathouse, amazing shells (the stupendously thin and fast crew boats), and a competitive spirit.

I spent many hours in that boathouse, working out on the ergs, rowing, and making friends.

I honestly don't remember how I ended up being recruited to be a coxswain for the lightweight male crew team.

It was likely some lucky accident, but it was an amazing opportunity that I wasn't going to pass up. I could work out during land training, and then join the men on the water, steering and coaching the eight rowers in my shell.

At one point I was assigned to a team led by an incredibly gruff second class.

Everything about him was intimidating.

He was tall and sinewy, had flaming red hair and a "prove it" attitude.

He was like a starving, pissed-off Viking.

Unsurprisingly, he appeared not particularly pleased to be teamed up with me (the "noob") in his boat.

Let me set up the awkwardness: in a crew shell, rowers face one direction (the opposite direction of where the shell is moving) and the coxswain sits in the end of the shell, the only person facing forward.

The Captain—Hangry Viking—was sitting mere inches from my face, and we couldn't escape each other.

I'll never forget how dismissive I felt he was of me initially.

I was a girl (I doubt he saw me as a woman).

I was just a Youngster (barely out of Plebehood).

Even with a military hairstyle and wearing standard-issue athletic gear, I was an outlier in my unmistakable femininity and natural warmth.

Perhaps most importantly, I wasn't the coxswain he was used to.

To him, I was unproven...and literally in his way.

Oh, did I mention that men's crew is divided into lightweight and heavyweight teams, and with the latter, the heavier and stronger you got, the better, but the lightweight team had to stay below a certain weight?

This meant the guys I was with were perpetually starving and yes, I'll say it: bitchy.

At first, I did my best to stay out of Hangry Viking's way as much as I could. Predictably, my AY steered me to spend time with the guys that I felt more comfortable with (the ones that I knew from other activities and who more readily accepted me).

I avoided Hangry Viking like the plague. I don't even think I looked him in the eye that much. But I knew that I was getting nowhere in my relationship with him by avoiding him.

The truth is, as Captain, he and I needed to work together. Earlier in the season, it didn't matter as much if we (literally) didn't see eye-to-eye.

However, as we got to the more important races, we needed to work together to shave off precious seconds and beat the indulged Ivy League teams.

I'm not quite sure what made me realize it, but one day in the shell, it just hit me: this Nordic Nightmare was giving off intimidating vibes, but he wasn't the problem in this situation. I lacked trust in myself.

Sure, he may have seemed scary, and appeared to take an overfunctioning posture with the rest of the team, but I had responsibility in this scenario too.

I didn't have to respond to all the anxious energy inside me, and out in the relationship network, with an under-functioning reciprocity. It just made me appear to lack confidence.

When I showed up this way, it was only natural that he had a hard time trusting me.

At the time, I thought he was a real jerk. But, thinking back, his posture made complete sense.

He needed me to be his partner. Because I was unsure of myself, I wasn't showing up as the confident co-leader he needed me to be.

I was doing what I needed to do as coxswain, and I thought that whatever else he demanded from me was unreasonable. In my mind, he was being unfairly mistrustful.

His questioning attitude affected me. Predictably, it made me question myself more. But it wasn't his responsibility to make me feel comfortable. He was there to row, and I was there to steer.

Further, his skepticism was logical: If I didn't have confidence in myself around him, then why should he?

I, presumably, know everything about myself that indicates whether I'm capable of keeping eight hungry college students out of cold, dirty water, not to mention preserving the physical integrity of a fragile and expensive shell, to say nothing of winning a race!

Only I have intimate knowledge of my genius. If I don't communicate this to him through my presence, how is he going to know it exists?

A PEEK BEHIND THE CURTAIN

There was so much anxious energy swirling in the relationship system that it made sense I showed symptoms. All the change and transition from Plebe year was a lot to process.

Plebes are in a perpetual (and intentional) underfunctioning position at the academy. It's hard to spend almost an entire year in that state and not start to place yourself in this position as a default.

We spent nearly a year having our (still very impressionable) brains wired in an extreme way. Then—poof—Herndon serves as this symbolic ritual to make it all go away.

As Youngsters we are respectable again.

Talk about a bizarre social reality.

I was also dealing with a lot internally. I was self-conscious because I didn't have years of coxswain experience. As a person with strong perfectionist tendencies, I was very anxious to be such a newbie.

I also was unsure about being a woman and non-engineer at the academy, and whether it was the right place for me. Of course, I didn't feel like anyone could understand these feelings, so I bottled them up.

All my anxieties about whether I belonged were being funneled into that relationship.

In my head, I initially saw Sven through the distortions of my anxious energy fueled AY. I was blaming him for making me feel insecure.

However, the situation was a lot more complicated than it appeared.

I was waiting for Slender Sven to make me feel worthy when that was my job. I wasn't responsible for all the anxious energy swirling around me. But I did have the ability to not accept AY's default response.

Only I could do it.

Once I remembered my worth, I could radiate this outward through my presence with others.

That's not to say that everyone would immediately and automatically accept me (that's an unrealistic desire if there ever was one!).

But those that could see me this way would. Typically, this is a far bigger group than we realize. We can't please everyone, but we can snag a significant group of fans by showing up in such a way that gives other people confidence that we belong there.

At the end of the day, Slender Sven was relying on me to do as damn good of a job as I possibly could, to keep him, me, and our teammates safe, and to (literally) steer us to victory.

I owed it to myself to show up with confidence.

So, what worked? I had two irresistible innate geniuses: a willingness to go all in and the ability to learn very quickly. I might make mistakes (and I did!) but I continued to get better. I was all in with him, morning after morning, I was learning every day, and getting better—rapidly.

Only I could choose to show up in the way that represented my full capabilities.

I didn't have decades of coxswain experience, but I knew enough to be pretty good. I also knew the only way that I was going to get better was to partner with Slender Sven.

When nineteen-year-old me realized what was going on around her, evaluated her patterns, and tried something new, something special happened: Sven started opening himself up to me, and taking on less of an overfunctioning posture with me and the team.

We became partners.

He would joke with me, playfully bantering using my pet nickname, and would share strategy and insight with me so that we could both get better.

I finally wasn't self-conscious anymore about being me. Because both he and I knew that—no matter the challenge, I was going to meet it.

How did he know this? Because I started acting in genius mode, being my true self: charming exterior, but with a spine of solid rebar (as I've been described by a former architect colleague).

The truth is people need us to show them our individual genius. They rely on us to bring our best selves to the task at hand, without getting caught up in anxious energy and AY. They also need us to believe that we have a "best self" before they believe it too.

This seems so obvious, yet how often do we think like this?

If we can't show up immediately with specialized technical competence, we need to at least have confidence in our capacity to learn and be persistent in the face of setbacks.

I had all these characteristics in spades, I just wasn't letting others in on this secret.

Others will not give us credit for something they can't see themselves.

OVERCOMING THE ILLUSION

There's a demonstrated phenomenon about trust: if a person is highly skeptical of themselves (and others), others will have a hard time trusting them in turn (Hogan Assessments 2012).

Harvard professor Frances Frei and Anne Morriss (2020b) discuss this "wobble" in their research on trust. They argue that others lose trust in us if we have a wobble (are a bit shaky) on either demonstrating our humanity (our authenticity), analytic abilities (what they call logic), or our commitment to the relationship (which they deem empathy).

Individuals may have a core wobble that shows up repeatedly in patterns with others. It may not be legitimate. Others may perceive a wobble in us that isn't accurate, based on a disconnect between who we really are—our genius—and how we are showing up for others.

This dynamic was occurring in my relationship with Slender Sven.

Because of my anxious energy, AY was making me too comfortable in an underfunctioning posture. I was showing up less than my true capabilities.

While it wasn't necessarily my fault, it was impacting my reputation. This was turning into an authenticity wobble for me in the eyes of Slender Sven. He may have thought I was misrepresenting some part of me.

Thinking back to my story, Slender Sven may have thought I was completely illegitimate as a coxswain, not because it was true, but because I appeared to lack confidence because of the many layers of anxious energy I was swimming in.

I stuck to the relationships I knew well, which certainly didn't build trust with him. He might have thought I was a real phony who may cause problems for him and the team.

Initially, I was so hung up on my lack of experience that I had forgotten I possessed a core set of incredible skills that were the raw materials for being an amazing coxswain. Since I couldn't see my potential, neither could he. Hence, I had an authenticity wobble around him.

I was withholding my true self by not demonstrating confidence in these raw skills that could someday make me an amazing coxswain.

Initially, this hampered my ability to gain the trust of the rowers and lead them.

Here's the good news, however. Once we take responsibility for the information we are broadcasting in our interactions with others—as I did when I had my stroke of insight in the shell that one day—then we bolster others' trust in us.

By taking responsibility for how we present ourselves to the world—despite how much anxious energy is swirling around us—we demonstrate our ability to see ourselves objectively, giving others confidence in our logic.

We also show up with confidence and humanity, bolstering our authenticity.

Further, we demonstrate to others how much commitment we have to the relationship, a clear sign of empathy.

All these actions build trust (Frei & Morriss 2020b)!

Trust expert Rachel Botsman (2018) defines trust as a confident relationship with the unknown. It's not a demand on others (or a demand others place on us), as we often conceptualize trust.

It's not binary, as we typically imagine (i.e., something you have permanently built with others, or that they have or haven't permanently built with you).

Rather, it is an active, dynamic process that requires regular actions to reinforce.

We all must do the work to reinforce this trust, on both sides of a relationship.

Our AY's survival obsession results in regular distortions that prematurely label others as untrustworthy, because of its over-rigid, completely unrealistic *inability of accepting any risk in relationships.*

When we don't think of others as trustworthy (or don't trust ourselves), they reciprocate and don't trust us as well.

This puts us at risk of cutting off, distancing, and taking an overfunctioning or underfunctioning posture in relationships (in a ham-handed attempt to deal with the anxious energy surrounding relationship risk). It's an illusion that human relationships can be risk free, and this is a barrier to establishing genuine trust with others.

Geniuses accept this risk. Psychotherapist and relationship guru Esther Perel (2021) notes that "trust is not a promise that we won't hurt each other. It's *acceptance of the risk that* we *will* hurt each other," and the self-assurance and confidence that, "if and when we do, we will come together to repair and to heal" (Perel 2021).

That's what happened with me and Slender Sven. We built trust with each other by overcoming our initial misunderstandings, and then sharing pieces of ourselves regularly, to demonstrate our willingness to accept this risk.

Perel (2021) notes that these little ways that we reinforce trust in our relationships serve an important role in actively maintaining trust.

Where does that self-assurance and confidence come from, the one that enables us to persist confidently as a separate self, capable of being connected to, and trusting others, without fearing that hurt from others will be an existential threat?

You got it, our genius. Our ability to be separate but connected. It fuels trust in ourselves, trust in others, and others' trust in us.

The truth is, we all have characteristics about us that we can't change—our race, gender, age, idiosyncrasies, even our innate gifts and talents—and we have characteristics that are capable of being upgraded: our learned talents and skills.

Others may choose to be skeptical of us no matter what; that is, essentially, their problem. They are missing out on the gifts we have.

Geniuses avoid unforced errors.

An unforced error in this instance would be us undermining our own trustworthiness because we lack confidence in ourselves, and we accept an underfunctioning posture. This lack of confidence broadcasts our skepticism of ourselves to others, essentially forcing them to mirror it back.

My friend Sven needed me to trust myself before he could trust me. And that starts with me—or rather, "I."

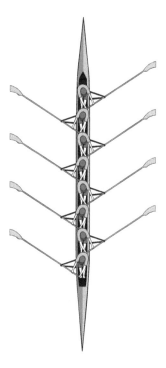

SET UP TO SPILL

———

"Up to ninety percent of bosses treat some subordinates as though they were part of an in-group, while they consign 'others' to an out-group [...] unfortunately for some subordinates, several studies show that bosses tend to make decisions about in-groups and out-groups even as early as five days into their relationships with employees" (Manzoni and Barsoux 1998).

It was day one of her new role, and Danielle was so excited that she barely slept a wink. She had recently been promoted to Senior Director, a result of her diligence and intelligence.

Now she had the opportunity of a lifetime, to work for a new boss who is a luminary in their industry, and to take over a large team with increased visibility and responsibility.

Danielle was meeting with this new boss, Heather, for coffee later that morning, and she wanted to make the most positive first impression that she could. She put on her smartest navy-blue suit, grabbed her bag, and was ready to take on the world.

Danielle arrived early at work that day, bristling with anticipation.

This was the first time she was meeting Heather, but she had enjoyed seeing her speak at an industry conference.

Heather was a direct hire, a rare occurrence at Danielle's organization, and was brought in as a Senior VP. Having built a similar division at her prior organization, she too was eager to prove she could replicate this success.

Danielle walked into the coffee shop, slightly jittery, and noticed Heather in the corner, hunched over a stack of papers. She approached Heather with confidence, extending her hand in warm greetings. Heather looked up and smiled, but her face didn't exactly convey warmth.

Danielle offered to grab coffee for both of them to give Heather a few more minutes with her paperwork. Heather agreed that would be a great idea, and Danielle set off to grab two cappuccinos.

Before too long Danielle was back at the table with Heather, setting down what felt to be unusually hot beverages.

Here is where our stories diverge.

Let's take a pause from the scene. Imagine that this moment, when Danielle returns to Heather's table, as a fork in the road, with two potential futures. We'll call these scenarios Danielle One and Danielle Two.

Let's play out Danielle One first. This is the "happy ever after" scenario, where Danielle One has an easy time charming her new boss Heather in the first ten minutes of their coffee. Danielle One begins the conversation by sharing a somewhat random fact about her past, and both she and Heather discover that they have a similar background.

Heather is surprised at how much she is enjoying this ordinary conversation, even though her stress level is through the roof. Danielle One puts her at ease. She seems so likeable, responsible, and intelligent. Danielle One's talents and competence will make it so much easier for Heather to demonstrate her capabilities to her own higher ups.

Within the first several weeks of working together, they face an unexpected challenge. No problem! Heather is incredibly impressed with Danielle One's ability to help her master her new role quickly, while helping her mount an effective response to this challenge.

This unexpected situation works in both Danielle One and Heather's favor, as their ability to put out the fire receives attention and kudos all the way to the CEO. It also gives them an opportunity to develop a close working and personal relationship.

As time goes on, Heather becomes more convinced that she will indeed be able to replicate her prior success at this new organization, particularly because of the talent and strengths of her new right-hand woman Danielle One.

Heather gives Danielle One greater autonomy to make decisions about her team and handle issues on her own. Danielle One blossoms under these conditions. She shares ideas that Heather will ultimately carry to the Executive Leadership Team, where she is quite proud to credit the intelligence and creativity of Danielle One.

Even when they disagree, Heather feels confident that Danielle One has a great head on her shoulders, and she rewards Heather with interesting stretch assignments to keep her engaged and interested. Heather has plans to retire early, and they spend a lot of time one-on-one. This provides Danielle One with the confidence to become Heather's worthy successor.

(And...scene).

Now let's rewind back to the coffee shop, and to Danielle Two. This is the "nightmare" scenario, where Danielle Two kicks off her relationship with an incredibly unfortunate mistake.

After returning from the barista station, Danielle Two sets the cappuccinos down on the table and takes her seat across the small table from Heather.

In an instant, her leather tote bag slips off her shoulder and knocks one of the coffee drinks squarely over Heather's papers. Disaster ensues when the messy coffee rapidly drips all over Heather's white pantsuit and onto her expensive tote.

Danielle Two stays as calm as possible, expertly deploying the stack of napkins she responsibly grabbed from the barista earlier. Heather and Danielle Two move quickly to sop up the pool of espresso and foam, but it's not enough to prevent the stains forming on Heather's jacket.

Now Heather is irritated. She doesn't want to cut this meeting short because she knows how important it is that they hit the ground running, but she has a presentation with her boss later today and will now have to build in time to change. She cannot show up to the C-Suite with a coffee stain!

Heather and Danielle Two hold a perfunctory meeting, with both women distracted by the mess. Due to the unaddressed awkwardness of the situation, they skip the opportunity to get to know each other personally.

They focus solely on discussing tactical issues to get through the first few weeks of working together. Heather's voice seems a bit harsh when she asks Danielle Two about the status of a few key projects.

The two women leave the meeting more stressed than they were earlier. Heather is left with the impression that her new report lacks confidence and is inexperienced. She wasn't impressed with Danielle's responses to her initial queries.

Because the two of them had no opportunity to get to know each other personally, Heather felt less motivation to give Danielle Two the benefit of the doubt that she was, indeed, capable of handling the work at the level Danielle Two needed to operate.

For her part, Danielle Two is not impressed with Heather either. She thought Heather handled her coffee accident with aplomb. (Danielle Two cringed when she relieved the memory of the spill.)

Otherwise, Heather appeared uncaring and distracted by her paperwork and meeting prep during their first meeting. Danielle's prior boss—who knew Heather well—had thought they would get along grandly, as they had much in common personally. However, neither of them had the opportunity to share this information, not in this meeting or in future interactions.

Several weeks after their meeting, Heather's stress and anxiety levels continue to rise. She begins to seriously doubt her ability to replicate her success at the previous organization, particularly since she is increasingly losing confidence in Danielle Two.

For her part, Danielle Two is still as likeable, responsible, and intelligent as Danielle One. After all, they *are* the same person. However, as time goes on, Danielle Two feels increasingly insecure about whether she is up to this new challenge and is confused by Heather's leadership style.

She begins to doubt herself. Heather keeps giving Danielle Two what appears to be routine assignments and is incredibly directive in how she expects the tasks to be completed.

A pattern hardens in between them where Heather is a stickler for details and Danielle Two, predictably, withdraws. The two women avoid each other, and their interactions became more and more stilted.

Heather doesn't appear interested in benefiting from Danielle Two's technical expertise or vast institutional knowledge. When their group faces an unexpected external challenge, Heather deals with it on her own.

She later tells Danielle Two that she felt it would be easier to handle it herself. Heather didn't know that Danielle Two faced a similar challenge in the past and could have handled the issue herself, taking pressure off Heather and lessening her immense workload.

Danielle Two's work has remained high quality, yet she is demoralized after Heather repeatedly points out small errors and typos, and demands to see final products before they are sent up the chain.

Danielle Two doesn't think that the role is what she expected it to be. She feels micromanaged, particularly because Heather inserts herself in her team decisions and never listens to her suggestions. Their conversations are tense and businesslike.

After a year of working with Heather, Danielle Two doesn't feel like she has any personal relationship with her supervisor. To her, it doesn't seem that they are gelling. Heather hasn't been forthcoming with feedback.

One day, Danielle Two overhears Heather speaking about her to a peer. Heather expresses doubts as to whether Danielle Two has what it takes to succeed in the organization beyond her current level. She also questions the organization's wisdom in valuing individuals like Danielle Two.

Heather's words—"I just don't know what other people see in her"—ring hot in Danielle Two's ears, convincing her that it was time to move on.

A PEEK BEHIND THE CURTAIN

This "Sliding Doors" scenario is based on composites of clients I've had over the years. I've known quite a few Heathers, Danielle Ones (and Danielle Twos).

Research indicates that leaders, despite their best intentions may be complicit in a team member's performance issues, by creating and reinforcing a dynamic wherein perceived under-performers are "Set Up to Fail" (Manzoni & Barsoux 1998).

The initial trigger could be as innocuous as spilled coffee, another minor personal issue (a less-than-stellar recommendation from a previous supervisor), or *even differences in values and social backgrounds.*

Often, these minor differences become magnified (as the supervisor's brain sees what it wants to see in the poor performer). This creates and then reinforces the set-up-to-fail relationship dynamic where seemingly weak or mediocre performers *live down* to their supervisor's low expectations.

Generally, they leave the organization, sometimes on their own volition, and sometimes after being forced out.

When managers *believe* their direct reports are talented and effective, their direct reports thrive accordingly. Turns out, the way that their managers treat their direct reports *impacts how they see themselves.*

The Set Up To Fail phenomenon can be viewed as a reverse Pygmalion Effect. Managers tend to expect that the performers they identify as weaker are *less motivated, more passive, less innovative and strategic, unlikely to suggest ideas, and as poor communicators who are weak in asserting their authority.*

When this categorical thinking takes hold, it becomes nearly impossible to change a manager's mind.

Further, after coming to premature closure about the perceived weak performers, they tend to separate them from the "High-Potentials" and treat them in a more controlling manner. This ultimately deprives those misclassified performers of confidence-building autonomy and makes them feel devalued.

They will sense these low expectations, their confidence will be undermined, and a downward spiral often commences. This doesn't just impact the outcasts; even high performers feel insecure about their position when their supervisors treat others in a controlling and hypercritical manner.

Their AYs are provoked by this treatment of others around them. Further, they are often expected to shoulder more of the work burden, inducing resentment of their supervisor and their peers. This additional responsibility doesn't belong to them and puts them at risk for burnout.

The Set Up to Fail phenomenon is a function of our AYs. We make decisions about people very quickly and can 'write people off' rapidly because of a minor mistake or difference, or even a person saying or doing something unimportant that we disagree with.

There's a simple explanation for this: our brains simply use up more energy (exhaust our internal resources) when we are around others we perceive are different than us (Barrett 2020).

AY is not happy with this additional brain expenditure, and misclassifications ensue (i.e., people are labeled as problems, rather than High-Potentials). Yoda is seeking for any information to cling to to quickly rid itself of the additional tax on its brain.

OVERCOMING THE ILLUSION

Agitated Yoda prompts us to make very quick assessments of others and situations. As discussed earlier, our brain operates in guesses, which we then create stories and reasons for later. This is a recipe for false impressions.

We can take a step back and question our default opinions about others, particularly snap judgments fueled by our AY.

It's valid to have clear standards based on substance, that is key to embodying our individual genius. However, it's quite hard, as a possessor of a human brain, to be truly objective about others.

Our brains deeply love to categorize others, and this categorization often portrays us (in our own minds) as heroes overcoming adversity, and others as the villains, or at least jokers, with serious character flaws.

This is an illusion based on our brain's warped view of the world. We have access inside our own minds and can clearly understand that our performance on any given day is comprised of millions of complex factors, and that we only control some of these factors.

When it comes to others, however, we often commit the *Fundamental Attribution Error* (Healy 2017).

True to its name, when under the influence of this thinking error, we erroneously believe that the mistakes of others are a result of their character flaws and evidence of their unworthiness, whereas we believe our mistakes are a result of the situations outside of our control (i.e., problems outside of us).

It's hard to recognize that this dynamic exists in our relationships. Not all clients want to hear it. Others, thankfully, have been grateful to look at their troubled relationships in a new light.

It's easier to prevent Set Up to Fail than to fix it. AY's guesses are sticky on both sides of the phenomenon (i.e., both Heather and Danielle), which can make it hard to repair relationship damage between them once established.

Open dialogue, clear and objective expectations, an acknowledgment of both parties' contributions, and a shared desire for a better relationship is necessary to attempt to reverse the dynamic once it's taken hold.

Finally, a willingness to change our minds, to upgrade our thinking—essentially, an ability to be adaptive—is a core element of individual genius.

Geniuses are constantly defining themselves. They don't have to come to a premature conclusion about others, either, even if anxious energy and togetherness pressure them to take positions on people based on superficial factors.

Geniuses take time to define for themselves their positions on others.

They resist default mode impressions and the temptation to prematurely throw others away.

They can see the genius in each person surrounding them.

OH, OH, OH I'M ON FIRE

––––

A current Google search produces over fifty-seven million results for "burnout."

Psychologist Herbert Freudenberger first conceptualized burnout in the 1970s, after studying factors that led to stress and self-sacrifice in doctors and nurses (IQWiG 2020).

By now we are all quite aware that burnout is extremely common in the helping professions and endemic in nearly all workplaces.

However, experts can't even agree on a clinical definition of burnout, or how common it is.

Judging by the popularity of the search term, we're all feeling the heat.

Freudenberg's work suggested that burnout might be a function of a self-sacrificial approach to life.

What do you think?

It's near statutorily required in a book like this to have a quiz, so let's explore further. In the last week, have you done/felt any of the following:

- *Agreed to do something that you didn't want to do?*
- *Anticipated the needs/desires of another person?*
- *Felt as though you were surrounded by helpless or needy adults?*
- *Worried more about another adult's problem than they worried themselves?*
- *Felt that you had all the answers about a particular situation?*
- *Did more about another adult's problem than they did themselves?*
- *Said yes when you wanted to say no?*
- *Actively solved another adult's problem that they could have solved themselves?*
- *Felt burnt-out or over-worked?*
- *Stopped listening before other adults finished speaking?*
- *Felt put upon "because you are the only one with the ideas around here?"*
- *Spoke more than other adults in group settings, potentially promoting groupthink?*
- *Played the role of saying too much in a conversation, advising/telling others what to do, preaching or teaching, or explaining unnecessarily?*
- *Continued making helpful suggestions to other people, even though the suggestions were being ignored?*
- *Felt guilty after saying no to someone?*
- *Protected or shielded others from the consequences of their own actions?*

- *Felt guilty about stating your own needs to another person?*
- *Had a hard time identifying what you really needed/ wanted?*
- *Blamed yourself when something went wrong?*
- *Contributed more than your fair share in a conversation with others?*
- *Ignored problems in your closest relationships?*

If you identified with quite a few of these, congratulations, you may be all-too-comfortable with taking an overfunctioning posture.

People in an overfunctioning posture chronically take on others' responsibility (Smith 2019). This may take the form of overhelping, overworking, and over caretaking. This posture may feel like it is squeezing the life out of us (Gilbert 2021).

Overfunctioning may also appear as knowing all the answers and dominating through constant talk (which may take the innocuous form of constant advice giving, teaching, or telling). This posture may overwhelm others (Gilbert 2021).

A proclivity for an overfunctioning posture might stem from the distortions of our AY. People who feel burnt out may be in a chronic overfunctioning posture.

Burnout was introduced to the world via an examination of doctors and nurses, two professions which just might be over-represented by those whose fundamental approach to others is over-caretaking and having all the answers (i.e., they might be particularly drawn to these professions).

Furthermore, these professions place very specific demands on their members to act this way, further fueling this burnout.

A caretaking approach is certainly not limited to individuals who are in the helping professions!

Burnout may occur in any person who—fueled by anxious energy in their relationship network—responds often with an overfunctioning approach to others. This is particularly true if they are also encouraged by the demands of their profession to be overly responsible.

As organizations face greater Thanos and Elephant threats, they have increased their demands on the workforce, expanding anxious energy in the relationship networks, and essentially sending a hand-engraved invite to the people in the system to be overly responsible.

No wonder burnout seems so common!

BURNOUT HURTS US AND OTHERS

The Mayo Clinic defines burnout as a "special type of work-related stress. A state of physical or emotional exhaustion that also involves a sense of reduced accomplishment and loss of personal identity."

Burnout affects both physical and mental health, prompting insomnia, high blood pressure, fatigue, heart disease, and even type-two diabetes. It can lead to substance abuse, worsen depression, and make us more vulnerable to illnesses.

My clients who feel the heat of burnout may appear cynical and overly critical of others. As indicated by the quiz above, they may feel as though they are the only ones with the answers and/or ideas, that they must do everything, and may find it impossible to delegate. Predictably, they may behave in an impatient manner, have a hard time concentrating, feel depleted, and may overly stress about work.

Sometimes, however, they disengage and go AWOL. Some people do a little bit of both.

Let's check Alejandro's temperature:

Alejandro is on fire. He leads a high-profile organization and cannot get a good night's rest to save his life. He feels solely responsible for making tough calls and has been continuously stressed about returning to the office post-pandemic. Primarily, he fears being criticized no matter what he chooses.

Alejandro rejects the idea of speaking to a therapist about his challenges, convinced he can deal better with the stress on his own. During his weekly one-on-one with his second in command, Amy, he spends the entire time sharing his stress and challenges.

This impacts Amy's professional growth, as this is the only face-to-face time she has with Alejandro, but she barely gets a word in edgewise with him. In their conversations, they somehow never get to the substantive issues she must discuss with him. Rather, he dumps his anxiety and stress on Amy, venting his troubles, yet refusing to see her as an equal partner in the conversation.

Alejandro believes that no one, not even Amy, can fully appreciate the stress he is under. Just months prior to the pandemic, the organization purchased brand-new office space, believing that an improved work environment would make everyone more productive and happier.

The organization paid top dollar for these fancy digs, yet very few want to return to the office. Alejandro is concerned that the board will question his decision-making skills because of the office situation. He feels solely responsible for this decision and its outcome.

For the past two years, Alejandro expects his leadership team to join him on a daily video conference, to discuss the challenges facing the organization. Alejandro still ends up making all the final decisions, but he feels slightly more comfortable during these meetings, like he's not alone, even if he is in charge.

He has noticed, however, that his team has increased their sniping and snarky comments to each other during these meetings. Their comments to each other in their leadership team group text chat have also become more critical, and direct text messages are tense.

Alejandro's team members avoid discussions of substantive issues with him. Rather, they often bring their complaints about each other to him, expecting him to fix the other person.

Exasperated, at one point he texts Amy, "I'm not your Daddy. I cannot fix your problems."

His team's performance is increasingly a distraction from Alejandro's long-term vision: single-handedly fixing the organization's issues.

Since taking over from his predecessor several years ago, Alejandro has obsessively involved himself in the activities in every single department.

He has inserted himself (and re-created) the organization's hiring processes, has changed policies set in place for decades, and has mandated across-the-board procedures that he designed, even if this uniformity precludes the achievement of efficient operations for some of the departments.

Alejandro is about as hands-on as a CEO can get. However, there are still areas where he fails to fully embrace his authority.

The stress of the past two years has exacerbated performance issues on his team. Rather than deal with difficult conversations directly, and embrace the responsibility that is his alone, he outsources feedback and coaching to external consultants.

After identifying a "problem" individual, Alejandro authorized an investigation into his division. In this case, Alejandro's indirect management approach worked, at least in the short term. While the investigation unearthed no bombshells, his much respected and experienced report couldn't take the stress and resigned.

Alejandro is truly a man on a mission.

He takes all the responsibility and actions, even though his team is highly intelligent and accomplished. He believes they are ultimately less equipped than he is and wishes they would just get on board or get out of the way.

When questioned about the substantive value of a decision, he struggles initially, then recovers and says, "I'm the boss and this is important to me. That's why we are doing it."

Alejandro demonstrates that a person can take an overfunctioning or underfunctioning posture in response to different challenges and situations. For some actions, Alejandro takes charge. For others, he gladly hands his responsibility over to others.

Alejandro knows he should be dealing with his reports in a more direct manner. It's just much easier for him to over-involve himself in every other aspect of the organization he runs.

A PEEK BEHIND THE CURTAIN

To comprehend how an overfunctioning posture may naturally lead to burnout, we first need to understand how it always occurs in equilibrium with a different force: an underfunctioning posture somewhere else in the relationship network (Chambers 2009).

The person taking the overfunctioning posture appears to respond to something that seems amiss in the relationship network, taking responsibility (beyond what is rightfully theirs) to fix it.

Their AY senses something is off and takes charge.

Whether motivated to help or control, the person in an over-functioning position will contribute more than their share to conversations and interactions. This overshadows everyone. Others have less opportunity to contribute their genius.

Sometimes this is a necessary posture to solve a problem in the short-term. However, when it becomes the default posture, it creates a long-standing dynamic over time that makes other people feel less important, and less capable (Gilbert 2006).

When one person always has the answers and the approach, everyone else will eventually contribute less and less of themselves, regardless of whether the person in an overfunctioning posture is doing it for glory or self-sacrifice.

Recall the "Set Up To Fail" syndrome? When a performer is treated as though they cannot handle the work, they generally fulfill these expectations.

Over time the impact on the person in overfunctioning posture is damaging. Often, both the person in the overfunctioning position, and those in underfunctioning positions will show burnout symptoms.

Furthermore, others may replicate this pattern in other parts of the network, with the person in underfunctioning posture carrying their "less than" approach to other roles, or taking on the overfunctioning posture in other relationships, to balance the system.

An overfunctioning approach can appear tyrannical, including shutting down dialogue, issuing directives, and cutting off debate with "because I say so." This may promote groupthink and under-delegation.

Those that harden in their dominator postures may keep loyal trusted advisors and cheerleaders around them at times.

From the outside, this loyalty may be admirable, and we may even believe that the dominator is altruistic, given their adoring fans. However, these supporters are giving blood and may be particularly prone to burnout.

Alejandro appears close to full-blown dominator posture and seems comfortable in an overfunctioning position.

He's not alone. I tend to take an overfunctioning posture when anxious energy runs rampant, and you might too. Both he and I strive for results, to be of service and value for others, and strongly feel the need to try to control and remove other's anxiety.

The supreme irony is that, for all the attempt to remove the anxiety out of these challenging and highly emotionally charged circumstances, the overfunctioning posture does the opposite. It introduces a huge amount of additional anxious energy to the relationship network.

Alejandro is dealing with a lot. He faces Thanos and Elephant threats, and his fair share of Narcissus threats. He's a Chief Executive in one of the most heightened times in recent history.

He doesn't feel he can trust his team and has a strong personal need to prove himself. Plus, he serves at the pleasure of demanding and arrogant Board members. Altogether, it's a recipe for classic over-functioning, and possibly, disaster.

We might look at Alejandro and think these pressures alone contribute to his burnout. They are indeed intense.

However, it is how he responds to these challenges that contributes the most to burnout.

Alejandro, like every person in an overfunctioning posture, responds to threats by taking more responsibility than is his within his relationship network (Chambers 2009).

He even takes responsibility for changing things that are outside of his control. This will foster burnout for sure!

OVERCOMING THE ILLUSION

If you're interested in trying a different approach, it makes sense to first understand where this posture is coming from.

Is someone else in your network taking a chronic underfunctioning position, or is there some larger dynamic occurring that you are reacting to (and your AY is compelling you to step up)?

What else is going on around you that could spark your proclivity for overfunctioning?

Resist the urge to blame yourself or others. Try to see this posture as a response to anxious energy in the environment.

The next step is to be curious and attempt to see how you might be overplaying your hand. You might ask yourself: *What is my responsibility and what is others? Whose responsibility am I taking for myself?*

Then, try to change the pattern by doing something different.

If you find yourself identifying with Alejandro, I'm not surprised. He is a common character in the business world.

We all tend to have patterns that emerge and re-emerge when we are surrounded by anxious energy. An overfunctioning pattern can have a strong negative impact on ourselves and others.

One of the most important things anyone can do is engage our curiosity about these patterns. Remember, we can only start doing something about these patterns if we can see them.

Some of us have an overfunctioning posture in some environments and around some people, or take on an under-functioning posture (acting helpless, requiring additional approval, not adding significant value) in other environments and around specific people.

Those with a competitive bent and a strong desire to demonstrate their power (like Alejandro) may not just take on an overfunctioning position but may also engage in conflict to distract themselves from anxious energy.

If we can change our part, even slightly, we interrupt a reciprocal cycle of overfunctioning (in me, Alejandro, and maybe even you).

In response, we will interrupt underfunctioning in others around us. Small changes in this pattern can produce big results for our organization and less burnout for all of us.

Geniuses are autonomous. The more autonomous a person is—the more comfortable they are with defining and living their lives according to their self-defined clear strategy—the less likely they respond to stress in patterned ways, including taking an overfunctioning posture.

That means we take less responsibility for others.

Geniuses are less reactive to anxious energy in networks and able to remain thoughtful (that is, respond based on their own values, principles, and beliefs) in the face of anxious energy, even when everyone else is freaking out!

When around others who are showing symptoms of anxious energy, geniuses feel a little less pull to mindlessly fix things for them or soothe them. They stay out of responsibilities and situations that aren't theirs.

They also resist the temptation to attack the problem (risking burnout when others can manage things just fine on their own), or to avoid the problem entirely.

Better to, as Smith (2019) notes, *approach* our problems with care not overconcern or under-concern. This prevents an overfunctioning posture.

Geniuses give others the space to handle their anxious energy (not trampling on their agency and autonomy) and feel less compelled to control or be controlled (protecting their own boundaries) by others.

Some of us may be more autonomous by nature, which is a real gift. Others may be less autonomous and inclined to operate in anxious energy-fueled patterns.

Even though we are humans who evolved to live in groups and as a result, we are all a little bit sensitive to getting our energy jumbled up with others, we don't have to accept where we are on the autonomy spectrum.

No human is autonomous one hundred percent of the time, but geniuses move more towards autonomy in their approach, protecting ourselves and others from the flames of burnout.

IN THE TANK

The door hinge closed gently, noiselessly, and then the space became completely black.

I laid backwards on top of the water, feeling its buoyancy prop and caress my ankles, the backs of my calves, all the way up to my back and shoulders. The water had a silky, almost viscous feel as it enveloped the backsides of my arms, elbows, and hands, reaching up to my neck and my gently bobbing head.

My hair splayed around me like Medusa, most of it spread out on top of the water like the rest of my body, with the high salt content keeping everything just above the surface.

I gently swished my arms through the water, cupping it in my hands, enjoying the challenge of pressing parts of my body down into the warm liquid. It was difficult! The salt water would gently force my entire being back to the surface.

My head stayed submerged just deep enough to fill my ears and prevent nearly all outside sound from being audible.

The sparse, gong-heavy soundtrack, piped in to soothe me into a meditative state, elegantly faded into no sound at all.

I was left with nothing but my own heartbeat. I lay still in the salt tank, all senses deprived yet bathed in the glow of extreme gratefulness. In a near transcendent state, I marvel at the fact that the average human heart beats more than two and a half billion times during a lifetime (NOVA 2021).

I think about how this is an opportunity to be with myself and myself only.

I roll my eyes about how predictably challenging it is for me to just relax and enjoy being in the moment without overthinking everything. I chuckle silently to myself; I knew all along that I would find this part challenging. I expected it.

I can just deal with it playfully, rather than engage in the silly and ironic act of *stressing over not being able to meditate*. I accept not being "enough" of a quiet mind.

I swish my body back and forth like a mermaid, gently testing the boundaries of my temporary salt tank home.

My hands press the sides as I float back and forth. The door is closed, as are my eyes most of the time. I do this to avoid provoking claustrophobia. Surprisingly, I'm just as comfortable with my eyes open. Occasionally, a few tiny flecks of light appear periodically, almost like stars in a gorgeous midnight sky.

I try to focus on the experience of floating, thinking about how I will ultimately describe it if someone asks. It feels like being on a swing, in that liminal space where you are flying through the air before the rope or chain jerks you back.

That in-between space is felt at all times, freeing you, supporting you, taking the space of gravity and letting your body just be.

Putting my arms above my head, I stretch out, farther, farther, farther until I can touch the wall above.

I push off it, whirring through the water sprightly for a short distance. My toes soften the landing on the far tank wall, and I gently push off again.

I do this back and forth for a while, enjoying its pleasant sensations. If I can't meditate, at least I can play! I explore the tank boundaries without any harm.

Once I'm out of the tank, showered, and dressed, I feel exhilarated. I have surprised myself. I have conquered that stomach-in-your-throat feeling I have long experienced in small spaces. It wasn't even that hard. I just needed to slow things down in my head and bring some curiosity and playfulness.

I originally signed up to visit the float tank because it's an amazing metaphor for our "I": a metal-and-plastic containment system for our genius.

Being in the tank made me think about the real importance of boundaries. As I playfully explored the metal sides of the tank, from top to bottom, side to side, I was thinking about boundaries.

As I laid on my back, my eyes would explore what looked like vast nothingness that—in full light—was a solid wall mere feet above my head. I couldn't see it, but I knew the top of the tank was there. It was solid. It was defined. It was enclosing me in one specific space. Defining where I was, and where I was not, at least for a time.

We humans don't exist in salt float tanks. We don't live in them. We don't do business in them. We are not inside our little tanks, solidly built, protecting, and defining us, and interacting and engaging with others inside their own little tanks.

That's a shame, because it sure beats having to create boundaries for ourselves, doesn't it?

SOLID FENCES CREATE FANTASTIC NEIGHBORS

Dr. Brene Brown (2018) notes that it's hard to get people excited about boundaries. Boundaries are hard, because once we define them, then we must live them. When that happens, other people may get upset.

You know what happens when other people get upset? Agitated Yoda Code Red.

So, unfortunately, we are naturally boundaryless. Sure, we have our human skinsuits, enveloping and protecting our inner organs, bones, and maintaining equilibrium of liquids, gases, and other organic elements of human bodies.

We also put on our fabric suits of armor, our clothes, shoes, and accessories, and place ourselves inside other material objects—our homes, offices, cars—to protect and represent ourselves to others.

Despite all these human-created barriers, we are still constantly bouncing off of each other, maybe not literally, but anxious energy-wise. Some of us have such boundary-violating relationships—true melding—we may exist in a perpetual state of *living and acting and being for each other* (Titelman 2014).

BOUNDARIES ENABLE GENIUS

Think this just happens in intimate relationships? That it couldn't possibly happen in the (supposed) buttoned-up world of work, where mature adults fully discharge their expected duties at the highest level possible while also respecting the social contract of interacting as professionals?

Dr. Brown (2018) recently identified the most challenging Narcissus threats that organizations face today, that severely hamper effective leadership functioning. This research encompasses an impressive amount of data, four hundred thousand independent data points, interviews spanning two decades, along with interviews with over one hundred and fifty global C-level leaders and other participants in her programs.

In my own work with thousands of executives, I've also repeatedly observed the problematic, AY-prompted behaviors listed here, which fuel Narcissus threats and anxious energy transfer throughout organizational systems:

- Avoidance of tough conversations, including avoiding honest, productive feedback. Related, a cultural norm of "nice and polite" which diminishes trust and engagement, and increases passive-aggressiveness, back-channeling, secrets, gossip, and what Dr. Brown calls the "dirty yes" (saying yes to someone's face but not actually complying) (*i.e., distance, blame, conflict, triangling*)

- Time management issues (i.e., *anxious energy-fueled overfunctioning*)

- Diminishing trust (i.e., *emotional distance)*

- People not taking smart risks or developing and sharing bold ideas to propel innovation; an absence of psychological safety or a fear of being put down or ridiculed for radical new ideas while groupthink and status quo thinking reign (i.e., *blame*)

- Teams getting stuck and defined by emotions, illusions, and anxious energy, particularly during setbacks, disappointments, and failures; leaders spending time reassuring team members who question their value, rather than directly dealing with issues or solving problems for customers or shareholders (i.e., *reassurance needs from melding*)

- An epidemic of shame and blame instead of promoting learning and holding others accountable (i.e., *blame)*

- Seeking quick fixes on difficult, complex, and long-standing issues, such as diversity and inclusion; seeking band-aid solutions that erode trust and prevent

meaningful change rather than open dialogue (*i.e.,*
operating according to AY*)*

- Rushing into ineffective or unsustainable short-term
  fixes for problems, rather than spending adequate
  time on problem identification and solving, perpetu-
  ating a cycle of fixing the wrong thing for the wrong
  reason (i.e., *operating according to* AY)

- Organizational values that are unclear, gauzy, and
  aspirational, as opposed to direct behaviors that can
  be measured and evaluated (*i.e., distance*)

- Fear and perfectionism being pervasive elements of
  the organizational culture (*i.e., chronic overfunctioning and underfunctioning postures, blame*)

I ask you simply: are any of these issues preventing
you and others from working as effectively as possible?
Do these things get in the way of substantive work at
your organization?

I see a whole lot of AYs, Narcissus threats, anxious energy
transfer, and Survival Six in that list.

POROUS BOUNDARIES AT WORK

When I'm in the saltwater float tank, I'm enveloped in my
own little world where it is easy to be comfortable, safe, and
defined. The walls on the bottom, sides, and tops of the tank
do this for me, along with the lock on the door outside.

Others down the hall are also in their own self-contained tanks, contained by their walls, their rooms, and their doors. We are blissfully coexisting, unaware of each other's existence.

Of course, being self-contained and completely cut-off means no possibility of interacting, no possibility of my talents combining with your talents produce some mega-genius outcomes.

Nobody wants that!

Incidentally, our talents combining is precisely the reason that relationships and organizations form in the first place. It's the reason that people work together, that organizations spend trillions of dollars on office space, and design their environments specifically for engagement and collaboration.

So the answer is not to just stay in our little self-contained tanks. The answer is to build virtual tanks—in our *minds*—to bolster our capacity for genius, and to be separate, yet still connected, to others.

Maybe a metaphorical tank doesn't work. How about thinking of boundaries as a VIP room, wherein you are the bouncer with the guest list (Cole n.d.)? You choose whose opinions, needs, and anxious energy you let behind your velvet rope.

Whether saltwater or bottle service, what is most important in boundaries is that we stay within ours and stay outside of others. Boundaries need to be mutually respected while we stay connected.

The key to this is not falling for AY's illusions. It's not falling into default mode. Boundaries are helpful here; they serve as the first line of defense for anxious energy.

Boundaries enable genius.

Genius is the capacity to separate ourselves from others, yet stay connected to them. To do that, we must know where our genius ends and others begins, and respect it. Every darn day.

The more we clarify and define the outlines of our metaphoric tanks and respect the outlines of others' metaphoric tanks, the more space we give others to be separate, yet connected to us: being their own genius.

The most amazing part about this is that it only takes one person to begin the process of clarifying and defining their metaphoric tank for others to willingly do the same for themselves (Smith 2019).

This work is empowering to others. It gives them space to be geniuses.

When we can be more genius, we are motivated, and others are too. Our boundaries, which is how our genius is operationalized, serve as a protective shield from melding and anxious energy. They protect us from this anxious energy in our networks.

Lest you think that our boundaries are somehow unpleasant for others, well, only because AY wants us to think so.

Boundaries give us space; boundaries give others space.

Who doesn't want more space for themselves?

This process also actively promotes collaboration, because the more I give myself my own psychological safety inside my own self-contained (brain) tank, the more I'm likely to engage with others confidently and effectively.

I can enjoy my interactions with others because I'm less likely (and they are less likely) to get drawn into a state of melding, because we are staying in our (brain) tank boundaries.

BUILD IT YOURSELF

Charlotte once said to me, "I need to remember that I'm not the problem around here." I agree wholeheartedly. She isn't. No one is. Remember, blame is lame.

It's vital that Charlotte remembers this as she does her best to cope with the anxious energy in her network. Recall her organization isn't the best with boundaries. Their logical system says one thing, but their default system means that people act another way in times of high anxious energy (which is all the time).

Charlotte isn't going to wait for her organization to change its ways. That hasn't happened in a century. She's building her own tank: defining her direction (separate from others), clarifying and living her boundaries, questioning her AY, and refusing to operate in default mode.

She is staying curious, getting comfortable with *seeing* the anxious energy circulating around the network, but refusing to contribute her own to the network. She's taking the time to understand her default mode, too, including seeing how she plays certain roles in relationship networks that are familiar and comfortable to her due to her early life experiences.

She's approaching all of this with a lightness. She takes her work seriously, but doesn't take herself, others, or all their anxious energy as seriously as she used to.

It's as if Charlotte is floating, just a bit, like I was in my tank.

Charlotte is giving herself space to be who she is, and with that, she is giving that space to others.

This is where we do our best work and get our best results.

We all deserve that.

You can have it in the tank.

CONCLUSION: USE YOUR ILLUSION—THERE'S ONLY "I" IN TEAM

———

She didn't know what was coming.

Several years ago, when our gliding nymph from the introduction took the stage and dazzled audiences with her athleticism and grace, one particular Thanos threat wasn't on her radar. She was just focused on being a magnificent and tremendously talented acrobat.

Who could have blamed her?

Her priority was overcoming gravity, not a pandemic.

Fast-forward to 2021. Cirque du Soleil was shuttered for *four hundred days*. Their revenues bottomed-out at zero, and the company laid off ninety-five percent of its workforce, close to five thousand people (Bilefsky 2021).

As you can imagine, working from home as an acrobat or trapeze artist is...impossible.

Even for those used to overcoming the impossible, sometimes nothing really can be done. When you are in the business of illusions, reality can be especially cruel.

I've thought about her every day for the better part of the last year. She's remained my acrobat muse as this manuscript has tumbled repeatedly through my head, just as she did on that death-defying ring several years ago.

Later, as I read more and more of the brain science, I'd want to track her down and find out how she's coping with this time. Cirque du Soleil suffered tremendously due to the pandemic, and the troupe's world-class acrobats and performers were losing their nerve from being forced out of the gym for the longest period of their performing lives.

The pandemic was a multi-level Thanos threat for members of the troupe: their lives were in danger from the virus, from the loss of the necessary practice that is essential for their death-defying feats to be relatively safe, and from the economic fallout of shuttered venues.

Our gorgeous acrobat would be forgiven for her anxious energy. It would indeed be rational if her Agitated Yoda were at twenty on a ten-point scale.

It would also make perfect sense if her head was filled with what Brene Brown (2018) calls our Shitty First Drafts (SFDs) (p. 259).

SFDs are a function of our AYs trying to guess our way through both imagined (and real) threats, and coming up with the first thing that comes to mind, which, if you learned anything from this book, will never be the full or real story.

That's why Dr. Brown calls them our SFDs: they are nearly always the worst-case scenarios because AY, (rightly) obsessed with our survival, can make every damn thing feel like a life-or-death situation.

They are illusions, or what Brown (2018) calls conspiracy theories. Yes, we are all operating according to conspiracy theories inside our own heads!

We know from Barrett's neuroscience that these SFDs are based on the brain's guesses. Brown (2018) notes that they are based on limited data.

Actually, they are based on made-up data.

They are creations from our brains, as impacted by the brains of other people (in the past and the present). Yet, they do serve a purpose: to create some type of coherent story to help AY deal with the threat in front of it.

But, as you know now, this isn't to help AY deal with the threat in a thoughtful, rational, and planned way for excellent results; it's just to get it to go away.

So, our flying goddess would be forgiven for having many SFDs about what is happening around her now. We all do it, automatically. At least hers would be informed by some actual Thanos and Elephant threats.

In my comfortable and familiar to me overfunctioning posture, my instinct is to tell her it was going to be okay. She'd build up her nerve and muscles again. She'd twirl again on the stage.

I'd reassure her that, despite the anxious energy swirling around her and the rest of us, it was a SFD that we wouldn't flock back to see her talent as soon as it was possible. We would be desperate to go out again, to enjoy her illusion, to escape our own, decidedly less exciting, illusions for a while.

I wanted to tell her this because of my own anxious energy. I don't really know what's going on in her head. Neither do you. Remember, it's probably best that we don't make assumptions.

After all, despite my AY-fueled desire to make it right for everyone, she is responsible for herself. She has incredible genius, and it's my job not to encroach on hers, or anyone else's for that matter.

The truth is, to be a genius, we need to be more responsible for ourselves, and decrease our responsibility for other people and what is rightfully theirs (Smith 2019).

Nevertheless, maybe she, and you, would benefit from what Charlotte has learned.

CHARLOTTE IS A GENIUS

Charlotte sees her AY as a function of her body budget. She pays attention to its survival freak-outs but doesn't accept them at face value. She takes the time to observe what is going on around her and tries to stay separate from and not as automatically affected by the anxious energy in her relationship network.

She observes the patterns in her relationship network (and sees her own patterns) and tries not take the default response or engage in the Survival Six.

She tries to stay curious about her own actions and those around her. She tries to be playful and retain a sense of humor.

She understands that she probably can't change people around her, so she'll work on herself instead.

She recognizes that defining herself (and embodying her genius) is a lifelong process. She can be close to others without being the same as them. She knows that being an individual **does not** mean she isn't close to or doesn't care about others.

GET COMFORTABLE WITH YOUR AY

Charlotte's successes notwithstanding (she has put in a lot of work), this process is a lifelong challenge. No one can be a separate genius one hundred percent of the time, so please don't be hard on yourself.

We are all constantly operating under the influence of our brain's guesses.

How you feel (i.e., your current emotional state, at any given moment) is not based on objective reality (something you can measure occurring outside of you) but is wholly based what is occurring inside your body.

Your brain guesses (based on your experiences and wiring from earlier in your life, and your life now) what is causing your body to feel the way it feels.

It then creates a story (a SFD!) to support this feeling (that appears to be based on an external person or event).

This process happens so quickly, and in your subconscious, you cannot sense it occurring. As a result, it appears to you (inside your brain) that others are impacting you emotionally.

However, this process is occurring through your own brain (and mind, which is impacted by your brain's AY, in concert with the AYs of others).

AY's predictions are solely about maximizing the body budget and staying alive, not being right about what is occurring outside of us. As a result, you may not want to completely trust its messaging.

One of the best things you can do in response to the way it makes us operate under the influence is to question whether your first response, your default pattern, is the right thing to do in response to any other person or situation.

Nobody in the business world wants to slow things down. However, if you've completed this book and still think you should trust your first interpretation of a situation or believe that your first answer to any problem or challenge is the right one, I've not done a very good job here.

If you want to get things (more) right, especially the things that really matter, take a little time to get more information, reassess, and then determine a response.

Not for nothing, Jeff Bezos of Amazon has referred to himself as the Chief Slowdown Officer (Bezos 2020).

Let's try a prototype. The next time you face a challenge at work, take an extra minute or two to question what you think is real, and you'll start getting results that appear to come from a genius, because they do!

Sometimes the best thing to do *is nothing.* At least, not right away.

Or, take some advice from Maria Konnikova (2020), and always have a reason for doing something, before you do it. That's her advice for not getting carried away by her AY's illusions and distortions.

Another reminder about the brain: concepts, affective realism, and social reality have been created by our brains to 'get along' with other brains for survival. These create our AYs.

They can result in everyday distortions of our perceptions.

Happily, when we are made aware of the created nature of these products-of-our-brains that our brains think exist for real (i.e., out in the world), we have the power to change/update them.

This isn't a moral "battle within." Remember, we debunked all that (sorry-not-sorry, Plato).

When we are young, our brain's guesses are instilled in us by others. Life experiences, and others—to this minute—continue to impact these guesses throughout our lives, which harden into patterns.

We are all operating under the influence of our AYs and default patterns. As humans with human brains, we cannot escape this. Relationship quality is impacted significantly by these default patterns. Results are impacted significantly by these patterns.

We can choose to not take the default and choose a different way of operating.

We can try a new way of being.

When we move beyond the default patterns, we see there is space for our genius, and for others' geniuses. Space for our angelic acrobat, for Charlotte, and Charlotte's boss, for Dominic, Julian, Victoria, me, my husband, Barb (and Kris), Jacob, Maria, Sven, Heather, Danielle, and Alejandro—for everyone.

There's space for you to be you.

This is how you foster collaboration. This is how you get amazing results. By default, people are thinking clearly about the Thanos *and* Elephant threats and are less obsessed with Narcissus threats.

They are contributing their best thinking to spur innovation and ingenuity, to meet the complex needs of organizations in the twenty-first century.

They aren't engaging in the Survival Six and creating more anxious energy and accelerating its transfer around the system.

In the end, we respect their *genius*. We respect your genius. Finally, and perhaps most importantly, *you* respect *your* genius.

Once you respect your genius, you think clearly, and when you add clear thinking into the network, everyone else does too.

You become the essential element: the "I" in team.

ACKNOWLEDGMENTS

In 1939, during a lecture at Columbia University, Alfred Hitchcock famously explained his use of the "MacGuffin" plot device:

"It might be a Scottish name, taken from a story about two men on a train. One man says, 'What's that package up there in the baggage rack?' And the other answers, 'Oh, that's a MacGuffin.' The first one asks, 'What's a MacGuffin?' 'Well,' the other man says, 'it's an apparatus for trapping lions in the Scottish Highlands.' The first man says, 'But there are no lions in the Scottish Highlands,' and the other one answers, 'Well then, that's no MacGuffin!' So, you see that a MacGuffin is actually nothing at all." (Bose 2020).

Even famous, non-Hitchcockian films feature a MacGuffin, often in the form of a random (typically somehow blessed or cursed) object upon which the main characters fixate, driving the true story of the film. As Hitchcock noted, a true MacGuffin, like the Holy Grail of early legends, is something that the characters care about, but which the audience (i.e., those with a bigger picture view) do not.

This book demonstrates how our relationships are filled with MacGuffins: things that we think are driving the action when something else is going on entirely.

If we're lucky, pursuit of the MacGuffin ends up spurring tremendous growth and transformation.

Since my early adulthood, friends, family members, colleagues, and clients have asked me, "When are you going to write a book?" It was the elusive MacGuffin seemingly missing from my life.

This questioning accelerated in the past few years, and thanks to the amazing Cady North and Eric Koester, I finally had my moment. I was going to be an author.

This book is a MacGuffin. Like all MacGuffins, it's important. They drive plot!

My Hero's Journey was no different than any other. The *journey of writing this book*—filled as it was with *many* ups and downs—ended up being one of the very best years of my life.

I'm forever grateful for this experience, and for the amazing people who came along. You have literally changed my life.

Thank you to my stalwart and absolutely stupendous supporters, the best *Team Genius* a writer could have:

Steven Hammons, Cady North, Lisa Freeman, Kendra Keller Ricks, Kelly Griffin, Sara Adkins, Aiko Smith, Marsha Carroll Lasiter, Angela Meyers, Erica Godwin, Erlita Shively, Bill

Colosimo, Robert Richardson, Dawn Platt, Karen Moloney, Karen Kelleher, Juliana Bellusci, David Rehrauer, Jessica Ault, Jennifer Copeland, Lisa (ASIL) Kaloczi, Lisa Pokoluk, Susana Vallelonga, Chelese Perry, Douglas Foote, Ashley Ridlon, Danielle McVey, Eric Koester, David Spadafore, Becky Troth, Kathleen Atkinson, Noel A. Nazario, Rebecca Wilson, Marco Palumbo, Corinne Champion, Ronald Robinson, Kevin Yousif, Anne Chasser, Brain Thibeau, Michael Pantschyschak, Alexandria McCombs, Melony Castro, Nancy Vislocky, Mersini Keller, Steve Hedberg, Briana Thibeau, Taleen Ghazarian, Stephanie Noel, Scott Dalessio, Hayley Tsukayama Thompson, Nita Patel, Lynn Herron, Russ Loecken, Lindsay O'Toole, Lynn E. Priddy, Thomas Pizzuti, Ruben Contreras, Joe Eulberg, Kathryn Brand, Stephen Ellis, Deborah Ruffins, Emily Pannell, Luba Kim-Reynolds, Venus Jenkins, Courtney Sapp, and Robert Radi.

Thanks also to Trudy Hale and Beau, for gracing the world with The Porches (and inspiring all of us via the amazing people who show up there every day).

Special thanks to Sohini Baliga, for your astounding editing skills and overall awesomeness. Our friendship is one of the best things to come out of the pandemic!

Efharistó pára polí to Andrew Demetriou, for your enthusiasm and introductions to awesome people. It's so wonderful to have you a part of my life outside the Commission!

Mucho appreciation to a most excellent *pal*, Gus Juneau. You constantly inspire me with your curiosity, openness, and humor. You are a superb dad and leader!

Toda Raba, my exceptionally wise and irreverent friend, Raymond Jasen. You make Fridays special, and I'll be forever grateful for your genius and contributions to mine.

And Brian Goldstein, you are an incredible human being and friend. You are the real deal in every way; you have earned every bit of your success, and the best is yet to come for you, guaranteed. From one genius to another: thank you for everything.

Thank you to my wonderful editors, Rachel (a real) Mensch and the amazing Camryn (Be Here Now) Privette. I literally couldn't do this without you; you've made the experience absolutely fabulous.

Much appreciation to my friends and amazing clients, past, present, and future. You are tremendous.

Thank you to Janice Grose: you set me on an amazing path. Amie Post: with you, I'm an archaeologist of precious jewels.

To my family, Mom, Dad, John, Dave and Sheital: you have given me immeasurable gifts. I love you very much.

To my extended family, you are appreciated for your genius. You'll always be a part of me.

Baron, my forever companion in ingenuity, along with Yukon, Justice, Salvatore, Molly, and Missy: forever Scooby Snacks for you all.

Juno and Benjamin Bear (and Rocco), your *genius* is precious, constant, and playful. You are the best.

And finally, Mr. Brr, you *are* the light of my life. I appreciate your genius more and more every day. It's no MacGuffin: it reveals itself like the most interesting (and playful) riddle, day after day. I'll take care of me for you if you'll take care of you for me—separate but connected. *I* love *you.*

APPENDIX

(INTRODUCTION: AERIAL, CANARIES, AND "WEIRD SCIENCE")

Barrett, Lisa Feldman. *Seven and a Half Lessons About the Brain*. Boston: Mariner, 2020.

Cirque Du Soleil: Best of Aerial. 2020. https://www.youtube.com/watch?v=bL3X1KZc48A.

Freifeld, Lorri. "2020 Training Industry Report." Training. November 17, 2020. https://trainingmag.com/2020-training-industry-report/.

Hughes, John. 1985. *Weird Science*. Universal Pictures.

Lerner, Harriet. *Dance of Anger: A Woman's Guide to Changing the Patterns of Intimate Relationships*. New York: William Morrow, 2014.

CHAPTER 1 (ILLUSIONS TO GET US THROUGH THE DAY)

Ariely, Dan. *Predictably Irrational: The Hidden Forces That Shape Our Decisions*. New York: Harper, 2009.

Barrett, Lisa Feldman. *How Emotions Are Made: The Secret Life of the Brain*. Boston: Mariner, 2017.

Barrett, Lisa Feldman. *Seven and a Half Lessons About the Brain*. Boston: Mariner, 2020.

Cooke, Thea. "The Hero's Journey in Advertising." Thearetical Concepts. February 4, 2019. https://www.thearetical.com/blog/the-heros-journey-in-advertising.

Duke, Annie. *Thinking in Bets: Making Smarter Decisions When You Don't Have All the Facts*. New York: Portfolio, 2018.

"How I Met Your Mother." 2005—2014. CBS.

Kahneman, Daniel. *Thinking, Fast and Slow.* New York: Farrar, Straus and Giroux, 2011.

Kegan, Robert and Lisa Laskow Lahey. *Immunity to Change: How to Overcome It and Unlock Potential in Yourself and Your Organization.* Cambridge, MA: Harvard Business School Press, 2009.

Kershner, Irvin. 1980. *Star Wars: Episode V—The Empire Strikes Back.*

Konnikova, Maria. *The Biggest Bluff: How I Learned to Pay Attention, Master Myself, and Win.*

New York: Penguin, 2020.

Konnikova, Maria. *The Confidence Game: Why We Fall for It ... Every Time.* New York: Penguin, 2016.

Skipper, Clay. 2020. "Lisa Feldman Barrett Says Your Brain Doesn't Work the Way You Think It Does." GQ. November 30, 2020. https://www.gq.com/story/lisa-feldman-barrett-interview.

Smith, Kathleen. *Everything Isn't Terrible: Conquer Your Insecurities, Interrupt Your Anxiety, and Finally Calm Down.* New York: Hachette, 2019.

CHAPTER 2 (THINKING IN NETWORKS)

Bowen, Murray. "Introduction" In *Understanding Organizations: Applications of Bowen Family Systems Theory,* edited by Ruth Riley Sagar and Kathleen Klaus Wiseman, Page vii-xii. Washington, D.C.: Bowen Georgetown Family Center, 1982.

Gilbert, Roberta. *Extraordinary Leadership: Thinking Systems, Making a Difference.* Lake Frederick, VA: Leading Systems Press, 2006.

Gilbert, Roberta. *Extraordinary Relationships: A New Way of Thinking about Human Interactions, Second Edition.* Lake Frederick, VA: Leading Systems Press, 2021.

Kerr, Kathleen. "An Overview of Bowen Theory and Organizations" In *Understanding Organizations: Applications of Bowen Family Systems Theory,* edited by Ruth Riley Sagar and Kathleen Klaus Wiseman, Page 1-8. Washington, D.C.: Bowen Georgetown Family Center, 1982.

Kerr, Michael E. *Bowen Theory's Secrets: Revealing the Hidden Life of Families.* New York: W. W. Norton & Company, 2019.

Kott, Katherine. "Applying Bowen Theory to Work Systems." *OD PRACTITIONER* 46 (3): 7., 2014.

Lerner, Harriet. *Dance of Anger: A Woman's Guide to Changing the Patterns of Intimate Relationships.* New York: William Morrow, 2014.

Miller, Jeffrey. *The Anxious Organization: Why Smart Companies Do Dumb Things.* Miami, FL: Vinculum Press, 2019.

Selva, Joaquín. 2021. "Codependency: What Are The Signs & How To Overcome It." Positive Psychology. September 13, 2021. https://positivepsychology.com/codependency-definition-signs-worksheets/.

Sobel, Bonnie. "Applications of Bowen Family Systems Theory to Organizational Systems" In *Understanding Organizations: Applications of Bowen Family Systems Theory*, edited by Ruth Riley Sagar and Kathleen Klaus Wiseman, Page 9-21. Washington, D.C.: Bowen Georgetown Family Center, 1982.

Smith, Kathleen. *Everything Isn't Terrible: Conquer Your Insecurities, Interrupt Your Anxiety, and Finally Calm Down.* New York: Hachette, 2019.

Wiseman, Kathleen. "Emotional Process in Organizations" In *Understanding Organizations: Applications of Bowen Family Systems Theory*, edited by Ruth Riley Sagar and Kathleen Klaus Wiseman, Page 33-46. Washington, D.C.: Bowen Georgetown Family Center, 1982.

CHAPTER 3 (AT LEAST WE AREN'T "NAKED AND AFRAID")

Kott, Katherine. "Applying Bowen Theory to Work Systems." *OD PRACTITIONER* 46 (3): 7. 2014.

Miller, Jeffrey. *The Anxious Organization: Why Smart Companies Do Dumb Things.* Miami, FL: Vinculum Press, 2019.

Russo, Anthony, and Joe Russo. 2018. *Avengers: Infinity War.* Walt Disney Studios Motion Pictures.

Survivor, CBS. "Sue's Famous Rat and Snake Speech." YouTube. June 17, 2007. https://www.youtube.com/watch?v=aBSMBf0MVHk.

CHAPTER 4 (TEAMWORK ISN'T SIMPLE, AND THAT IS TERRIFIC)

Lencioni, Patrick. *The Five Dysfunctions of a Team: A Leadership Fable.* San Francisco, CA: Jossey-Bass, 2002.

Russo, Anthony, and Joe Russo. 2018. *Avengers: Infinity War.* Walt Disney Studios Motion Pictures.

CHAPTER 5 (INTERLUDE: INDIVIDUAL GENIUS)

Bowen, Murray. *Family therapy in clinical practice.* New York: Jason Aronson, 1978.

Kouzes, James and Barry Pozner. *Credibility: How Leaders Gain and Lose It, Why People Demand It.* San Francisco, CA: Jossey-Bass, 2011.

Lerner, Harriet. *Dance of Anger: A Woman's Guide to Changing the Patterns of Intimate Relationships.* New York: William Morrow, 2014.

McEwen, Bruce. *The End of Stress as We Know It*. Joseph Henry Press/The Dana Press. 2016.

McKeown, Greg. *Essentialism: The Disciplined Pursuit of Less*. Redfern, New South Wales, Australia: Currency, 2014.

"The Big Bang Theory." 2007—2019. CBS.

Titleman, Peter. *Differentiation of Self: Bowen Family Systems Theory Perspectives*. Abingdon, Oxfordshire, England, UK: Routledge, 2014.

Van Sant, Gus. 1997. *Good Will Hunting*. Miramax Films.

"We Take a Look at the Etymology behind the Word 'genius.'" 2016. Blog. Collins Dictionary. July 14, 2016. https://blog.collinsdictionary.com/language-lovers/we-take-a-look-at-the-etymology-behind-the-word-genius/.

CHAPTER 6 (A REAL BOY)

Disney, Walt. 1940. *Pinnocchio*. RKO Radio Pictures.

Gilbert, Roberta. *Extraordinary Leadership: Thinking Systems, Making a Difference*. Lake Frederick, VA: Leading Systems Press, 2006.

"How I Met Your Mother." 2005—2014. CBS.

King, Stephen. *Misery*. New York: Viking, 1987.

CHAPTER 7 (SCOOBY SNACKS)

Frei, Frances X., and Anne Morriss. *Unleashed: The Unapologetic Leader's Guide to Empowering Everyone Around You*. Harvard Business Review Press 2020a.

Mitic, I. "15 Insightful Pet Spending Statistics (2021)." Fortunly. October 12, 2021. https://fortunly.com/statistics/pet-spending-statistics/.

Pflaum, Nadia. "John Kasich Misquotes Truman on Dogs, Wins Ohio Anyway." Politifact. March 17, 2016. https://www.politifact.com/factchecks/2016/mar/17/john-kasich/john-kasich-misquotes-truman-wins-ohio-anyway/.

Smith, Kathleen. *Everything Isn't Terrible: Conquer Your Insecurities, Interrupt Your Anxiety, and Finally Calm Down*. New York: Hachette, 2019.

Smith, Larry. "Larry Smith: Why You Will Fail to Have a Great Career." TED. November 2011. https://www.ted.com/talks/larry_smith_why_you_will_fail_to_have_a_great_career/transcript?language=en.

Urban, Tim. "Why You Should Stop Caring What Other People Think (Taming the Mammoth)." Wait But Why. June 13, 2014. https://waitbutwhy.com/2014/06/taming-mammoth-let-peoples-opinions-run-life.html.

"What Is Pot Committed in Poker?" n.d. Upswing Poker. Accessed October 20, 2021. https://upswingpoker.com/glossary/pot-committed/.

CHAPTER 8 (MRS. O'LEARY AND THE MISATTRIBUTION)
Barrett, Lisa Feldman. *How Emotions Are Made: The Secret Life of the Brain.* Boston: Mariner, 2017.

Gilbert, Roberta. *Extraordinary Leadership: Thinking Systems, Making a Difference.* Lake Frederick, VA: Leading Systems Press, 2006.

McKay, Adam. 2004. Anchorman: The Legend of Ron Burgundy. DreamWorks Pictures.

Schons, Mary. "The Chicago Fire of 1871 and the 'Great Rebuilding.'" National Geographic. January 25, 2011. https://www.nationalgeographic.org/article/chicago-fire-1871-and-great-rebuilding/.

CHAPTER 9 (HELL IS OTHER PEOPLE)
Collins, Jim. n.d. "Jim Collins—Concepts—The Stockdale Paradox." Jim Collins. Accessed October 17, 2021. https://www.jimcollins.com/concepts/Stockdale-Concept.html.

Lerner, Harriet. *Dance of Anger: A Woman's Guide to Changing the Patterns of Intimate Relationships.* New York: William Morrow, 2014.

Tarantino, Quentin. 1994. *Pulp Fiction.* Miramax Films.

CHAPTER 10 (SLENDER SVEN AND MY UNFORCED ERROR)
Botsman, Rachel. "Trust-Thinkers. What Does It Really Mean to Trust?" Medium. July 26, 2018. https://medium.com/@rachelbotsman/trust-thinkers-72ec78ec3b59.

Frei, Frances X., and Anne Morriss. "Begin with Trust." Harvard Business Review. June 2020b. https://hbr.org/2020/05/begin-with-trust.

"Meet the Skeptic." 2012. Blog. Hogan Assessments. February 16, 2012. https://www.hoganassessments.com/blog/meet-the-skeptic/.

"Noob Definition & Meaning | Dictionary.Com." n.d. Reference. Dictionary. Accessed October 20, 2021. https://www.dictionary.com/browse/noob.

Perel, Esther. 2021. "Risk Taking and Trust—Letters from Esther Perel." YouTube. May 19, 2021.
https://www.youtube.com/watch?v=cnLnu3emoPU.

CHAPTER 11 (SET UP TO SPILL)

Healy, Patrick. "Fundamental Attribution Error: What It Is & How to Avoid It—Harvard Business School Online." Harvard Business School. June 8, 2017.
https://online.hbs.edu/blog/post/the-fundamental-attribution-error.

Manzoni, Jean-Francois, and Jean-Louis Barsoux. "The Set-Up-To-Fail Syndrome." Harvard Business Review. April 1998.
https://hbr.org/1998/03/the-set-up-to-fail-syndrome.

CHAPTER 12 (OH, OH, OH, I'M ON FIRE)

Chambers, Megan F. Nothing Is as Practical as a Good Theory: Bowen Theory and the Workplace—a Personal Application, *Australian and New Zealand Journal of Family Therapy*, 2009.

"Depression: What Is Burnout?" NCBI—Bookshelf. June 18, 2020.
https://www.ncbi.nlm.nih.gov/books/NBK279286/.

Gilbert, Roberta. *Extraordinary Relationships: A New Way of Thinking about Human Interactions, Second Edition*. Lake Frederick, VA: Leading Systems Press, 2021.

Russo, Anthony, and Joe Russo. 2018. *Avengers: Infinity War*. Walt Disney Studios Motion Pictures.

Smith, Kathleen. *Everything Isn't Terrible: Conquer Your Insecurities, Interrupt Your Anxiety, and Finally Calm Down*. New York: Hachette, 2019.

Staff. "Job Burnout: How to Spot It and Take Action." Mayo Clinic. June 5, 2021.
https://www.mayoclinic.org/healthy-lifestyle/adult-health/in-depth/burnout/art-20046642.

CHAPTER 13 (IN THE TANK)

Brown, Brene. *Dare to Lead: Brave Work. Tough Conversations. Whole Hearts*. New York: Random House, 2018.

Cole, Terri. "Do You Know Your Boundary Rights?" Terri Cole. 2021.
https://www.terricole.com/boundaryboss-bill-of-rights/.

"Estimating the Size of the Commercial Real Estate Market in the US | Nareit." n.d. REIT. Accessed October 17, 2021.
https://www.reit.com/data-research/research/nareit-research/estimating-size-commercial-real-estate-market-us.

"NOVA Online | Cut to the Heart | Map of the Human Heart | Amazing Heart Facts." n.d. PBS. Accessed October 17, 2021. https://www.pbs.org/wgbh/nova/heart/heartfacts.html.

Smith, Kathleen. *Everything Isn't Terrible: Conquer Your Insecurities, Interrupt Your Anxiety, and Finally Calm Down*. New York: Hachette, 2019.

Titleman, Peter. *Differentiation of Self: Bowen Family Systems Theory Perspectives.* Abingdon, Oxfordshire, England, UK: Routledge, 2014.

CHAPTER 14 (CONCLUSION: USE YOUR ILLUSION—THERE'S ONLY "I" IN TEAM)

Bezos, J., and W. Isaacson. 2020. *Invent and Wander: The Collected Writings of Jeff Bezos, With an Introduction by Walter Isaacson*. Harvard Business Review Press.

Bilefsky, Dan. "Cirque Du Soleil's Return Could Be Its Most Challenging Feat Yet." The New York Times. May 9, 2021. https://www.nytimes.com/2021/05/09/world/canada/cirque-du-soleil-returns.html.

Brown, Brene. *Dare to Lead: Brave Work. Tough Conversations. Whole Hearts.* New York: Random House, 2018.

Konnikova, Maria. *The Biggest Bluff: How I Learned to Pay Attention, Master Myself, and Win.*

New York: Penguin, 2020.

Russo, Anthony, and Joe Russo. 2018. *Avengers: Infinity War.* Walt Disney Studios Motion Pictures.

Smith, Kathleen. *Everything Isn't Terrible: Conquer Your Insecurities, Interrupt Your Anxiety, and Finally Calm Down*. New York: Hachette, 2019.

ACKNOWLEDGEMENTS

Bose, Swapnil Dhruv. "Alfred Hitchcock Explains Vital Plot Device 'The MacGuffin'." Far Out Magazine. March 2021. https://faroutmagazine.co.uk/alfred-hitchcock-the-macguffin-explanation/.

Survival S. x
- Narcissus
- Elephant
- Thanos